"[Jesus] understands human sufferings,
he has shown the face of God's mercy,
and he has bent down to heal body and
soul. This is Jesus. This is his heart."

—Pope Francis

the CHURCH *of* MERCY

A VISION FOR THE CHURCH

BY

POPE FRANCIS

LOYOLA PRESS.
A JESUIT MINISTRY
Chicago

LOYOLA PRESS.
A JESUIT MINISTRY

3441 N. Ashland Avenue
Chicago, Illinois 60657
(800) 621-1008
www.loyolapress.com

First published in English in 2014 by
Darton, Longman and Todd Ltd
1 Spencer Court
140–142 Wandsworth High Street
London SW18 4JJ

Published in Italian in 2014 by Edizione San Paolo
Piazza Soncino 5, 20092 Cinisello Balsamo (Mi), Italy

© 2014 Periodici San Paolo s.r.l.
Via Giotto, 36–20145 Milano
www.famigliacristiana.it

© 2014 Edizioni San Paolo s.r.l.
Piazza Soncino, 5–20092 Cinisello Balsamo (Milano)
www.edizionisanpaolo.it

© 2014 Libreria Editrice Vaticana
00120 Città del Vaticano
www.libreriaeditricevaticana.com

Scripture quotations are from the *New American Bible* 2002 and *The New Jerusalem Bible* 1985. *New American Bible*, © 2002 by United States Conference of Catholic Bishops, Washington, D.C. *The New Jerusalem Bible* © 1985 by Darton, Longman & Todd Ltd and Doubleday, a division of Bantam Doubleday Dell Publishing Group, Inc.

Cover art credit: Photo of Pope Francis, AFP/Pool/AFP Collection/Getty Images, texture photos, Miro Novak/Shutterstock, Kaspri/Shutterstock.

Hardcover

ISBN-13: 978-0-8294-4168-0
ISBN-10: 0-8294-4168-9

Paperback

ISBN-13: 978-0-8294-4170-3
ISBN-10: 0-8294-4170-0
Library of Congress Control Number: 2014934036

Printed in the United States of America.
14 15 16 17 18 19 Bang 10 9 8 7 6 5 4 3 2 1

CONTENTS

Foreword

Who? That was the question many found themselves asking on March 13, 2013, following the announcement that Cardinal Jorge Mario Bergoglio had been elected Pope. The election of the former Archbishop of Buenos Aires surprised a great number of us. However, once Pope Francis appeared on the balcony with that lovely smile, his simplicity and humility evident, the initial surprise soon gave way to certainty that this man was God's choice. Our new Holy Father's first act (after cracking a joke about the cardinals having to go to the ends of the earth to find a new Bishop of Rome) was to ask us to pray for him before he bestowed his blessing upon us. The silence was so powerful! Pope Francis is now well-known and much-loved throughout the world, not just by Catholics, but by very many others besides—including those who profess no religious allegiance. Such is the remarkably positive impression he has made after less than a year in office.

At the Mass of Thanksgiving for the election of Pope Francis in Westminster Cathedral the day after, I quoted some words he had written while he was still Archbishop of Buenos Aires: "Only someone who has encountered mercy, who has been caressed by the tenderness of mercy, is happy and comfortable with the Lord." The mission of Pope Francis is, I said, to enable us to experience "the caress of the mercy of Jesus Christ on my sin." From our encounter with mercy, from our experience of the tender caress of Jesus, a profound joy and hope is born in our hearts. It is a joy and hope that grants us the courage to go out from ourselves to share with others the delight of meeting Jesus. We are not afraid to go even to the furthest edges of human existence because the Lord walks with us and, indeed, before us. The motto of Pope Francis, taken from the Venerable Bede's commentary on the call of St. Matthew, *miserando atque eligendo*, means lowly but chosen—literally in Latin "by having mercy, by choosing him." This is our motto too. Having been touched by Jesus' mercy and chosen by him, we are sent out, sinners that we are, to be heralds, missionary disciples, of divine mercy. Our desire is the same as that of Pope Francis: that everyone experiences the Church as merciful.

The Church of Mercy will, I am sure, help our common desire to be realized. It is a most welcome publication. This collection of texts, taken from the Holy Father's homilies, addresses, and official teaching documents, shows just how admirably Pope Francis can find a turn of phrase that catches our attention, engages our imaginations, and moves us to action—and even makes us laugh out loud! But, as this collection also shows, these are no shallow sound bites. No, there is real substance behind them. Pope Francis's words reflect his profound immersion in the sacred Scriptures, the Fathers, and the witness of his predecessors, not least that of Benedict XVI. They are words whose meaning we find most effectively conveyed in the gestures of Pope Francis, gestures flowing from a life of prayer.

Prayer must enjoy primacy. The first duty of a bishop, the Pope reminds me, is to pray, then to proclaim the Gospel by my life and deeds. Evangelization *is* the mission of a Church that welcomes all and is willing to journey "to the edges" as the servant of those dwelling in poverty, both material and spiritual. Such a universal mission demands that we are a Church ceaselessly praying to the Holy Spirit. Our need to be guided by the Holy Spirit is pivotal to understanding everything Pope Francis proclaims in word and action. We are called and sent out to be Spirit-filled evangelizers. It is the Holy Spirit who fixes our gaze on Jesus, who assures us that Jesus' gaze is always upon us, who each day makes wonderfully new our relationship with Jesus.

This is the true radicalism of the Pope's message: Jesus must always be at the center. Intimacy with him is the heart of all we do and are, and it is the heart into which we wish to welcome others. Our inspiration—the treasure we long to share—is the joy of the Gospel of Jesus Christ. We do not look to sociology, philosophy, or any political ideology to explain why we must be a poor Church for the poor. We look to Christ, who reveals to us the face of God, the Father of mercies. To look to Christ is to look to the poor. To reach out to the poor is to reach out and touch the flesh of Christ. We do so with humility. For from those "on the edges" we have so much to learn.

Bishops, priests, deacons, all pastoral workers, every Christian, and especially young people—for whom Pope Francis has such obvious love—will find this book a source of great encouragement and consolation. So, too, will they find it extremely challenging! The Pope asks penetrating questions that catapult us out of any self-centered complacency into which we may have fallen. I frequently found myself using the text as an examination of conscience. Yet never was it a cause for despair. For we are reassured that God's patient mercy is infinitely greater than our sinfulness. God will never abandon us. This is a beautiful truth for everyone to hear. Therefore I hope this book will reach as wide a readership as possible.

Finally, Pope Francis invites us to take Mary as our example. Mary, woman of faith, hope, and love; Mary who listens prayerfully; Mary ever guided by the Holy Spirit; Mary always obedient to the Father's will; Mary who teaches us how to give flesh to Christ in our world, how to be the "Church of Mercy." In so doing, Mary the Mother of Mercy is also Mother of our Joy.

Vincent Cardinal Nichols

Vincent Cardinal Nichols is the Archbishop of Westminster
and head of the Roman Catholic Church in England and Wales.
On February 22, 2014, Pope Francis appointed Nichols
to the Sacred College of Cardinals.

Preface

It is only a year since Pope Francis began his pontificate, but his pastoral plans for the Church seem already very well-defined. From the start his words, gestures, and decisions have clearly shown the style and direction he intends his teaching magisterium to have. As time has gone by, his vision has extended and consolidated, opening up new horizons for the Church's life. In the apostolic exhortation *Evangelii gaudium* (24 November 2013), the pope set out the main goals of his plan, thus writing the Church's "Magna Carta" for the coming years. In its broad vision and rich contents, the exhortation resembles an encyclical letter. His words are all about the missionary face of the Church and, most of all, the new way of "being Church" that the pope would like the Church to adopt through a more authentic proclamation and witness to the Gospel by Christians.

Obviously, Pope Francis is well aware that the Church's poor fishermen have fragile boats and much-mended nets, and that, despite their efforts, they are often not able to catch anything. This is what he reminded the Brazilian bishops of in the Document of Aparecida (27 July 2013). Since God's will underlies everything, Pope Francis also knows well that the strength of the Church doesn't depend on its members and their capabilities, because they are both weak and inadequate. Rather its strength "is hidden in the deep water of God, where it is summoned to cast its nets."

How these nets should be cast is the focus of Pope Francis's apostolic preaching and mission. This collection of papers is basically the framework that defines the pastoral and ecclesial program. The keyword of his program, which signposts the way, is sealed in the title: *mercy*. Indeed, Francis's Church wants to be recognized first of all as the house of mercy that, between human weakness and God's patience, welcomes and helps find the "good news" of the great Christian hope. Whoever reaches this house and surrenders to God's mercy will not only cease to feel lonely and abandoned but will also discover a fuller existence, lit up by faith and the love of the living God—Christ who died, rose again, and now is alive in his Church. Whoever meets him and stays with him learns the grammar of a Christian life and, first of all, the need for forgiveness and reconciliation, for brotherly and sisterly love, which Christians must spread in the world as joyful witnesses to God's mercy. Not only do they need to show understanding and sympathy, and remain close to those who endure moral or physical sufferings, but they also need to become people who truly and deeply bear others' pains and difficulties with the greatest tenderness, magnanimity, and solidarity, and to be people who offer solace, hope, and encouragement to keep on walking on the path of the Lord of life.

The good news of Christianity is Christ himself. His words give salvation and life because he is shelter and life. In the Church, people believe in this truth of faith, and all who adopt it as the fullness of the sacramental life find their direction and support to live as Christians, whose goal is holiness. The steps toward this finishing line are listening, proclaiming, and witnessing to the Gospel. According to Pope Francis's theology, full-time Christians don't sit down to admire their faith in the reflection of a mirror, nor talk about it over dinner, but they come out of themselves, embrace their cross with courage and walk the streets to share with everybody the joy of the Gospel. Pope Francis never gets tired of telling everyone that evangelizing is conversion, going out, and walking. The first to be summoned are the priests, "anointed to anoint," whose duties are to welcome and to serve. They are asked not to be afraid to go to the furthest boundaries and outskirts of human existence to meet the poor, the marginalized, and the least.

Those who are materially, spiritually, and humanly poor are not the focus of special attention because they are an economic, social, or pastoral problem, but because the loving God, poor among the poor, reserved for them a privileged place in Christ's life and ministry. The "poor Church for the poor" of Pope Francis is a principle that defines in an evangelistic sense the choice of poverty and service to the poor, thus continuing the wonderful story of a loving Church that throughout the centuries has been a way to liberation, inclusion, and promotion for the poor, following Christ's idea of liberty and love. Christ indeed offers not only generous, practical, and constant solidarity, but he also actively affirms human dignity, pursues justice, and builds a civilization that is effectively "human."

In this context of pastoral vision for the Church, Pope Francis's idea of human beings in relation to society is embedded. His distinctive emphasis runs parallel to and interacts with the rest. His strong and direct speech shakes consciences to strike the "hardened" heart of a society whose culture is not open to the idea of coming together for the common good. These are the premises for a neighborly and peaceful existence. It is not possible to move forward toward a better world until such idols as power, money, corruption, careerism, selfishness, indifference, or, to sum up, "the spirit of the world," are demolished.

These concepts are clearly explained also in *Evangelii gaudium*, which reveals to us both the bad habits that need to be abandoned and the pastoral priorities in the public life of the Church. In this effort the pope leads the way by word and sets the pace, which quickens day by day. His aim is to let people understand that an authentic Christianity, faithful to the spirit of the Gospel, is not achievable if the people in Christian communities have a weary and half-asleep faith, without any thrill of excitement, a faith shut up within the walls of their hearts or church buildings. This is the danger that might materialize if the Church grows old and accustomed to caring only about itself rather than flinging open its doors and facing the challenges of the world. It doesn't matter if the Church sometimes fails on the way. This is why Pope Francis keeps sending out warnings that heavy-handedness, intransigence, hypocrisy, and other shortcomings need to be abolished because they undermine Christian credibility. He is determined to reform and renew the Church so that it becomes better equipped to pursue its goals, with all that that involves.

In short, the life of the Church needs to be cleansed, renewed, and revitalized. This requires an ecclesial and pastoral discernment that enables the Church to rediscover the essence of its missionary mandate, in the light of the Holy Spirit and with the intercession of Mary, mother of the task of proclaiming the Gospel.

Giuliano Vigini

Giuliano Vigini is a Professor at The Catholic University of Milan and has edited books by Pope Paul VI; Cardinal Carlo Maria Martini; Pope Benedict 16th; and Pope Francis.

PART ONE

The Good News of Christ

1

The Embrace of God's Mercy

*Homily for the Mass for the Possession of the Chair of the
Bishop of Rome, 7 April 2013*

What a beautiful truth of faith this is for our lives: the mercy of God! God's love for us is so great, so deep; it is an unfailing love, one that always takes us by the hand and supports us, lifts us up, and leads us on.

In the Gospel of John (20:19–28), the apostle Thomas personally experiences this mercy of God, which has a concrete face: the face of Jesus, the risen Jesus. Thomas does not believe it when the other apostles tell him, "We have seen the Lord." It isn't enough for him that Jesus had foretold it, promised it: "On the third day I will rise." He wants to see, he wants to put his hand in the place of the nails and in Jesus' side. And how does Jesus react? With *patience*: Jesus does not abandon Thomas in his stubborn unbelief; he gives him a week's time. He does not close the door; he waits. And Thomas acknowledges his own poverty, his little faith: "My Lord and my God!" With this simple yet faith-filled invocation, he responds to Jesus' patience. He lets himself be enveloped by divine mercy; he sees it before his eyes, in the wounds of Christ's hands and feet and in his open side, and he discovers trust. He is a new man, no longer an unbeliever, but a believer.

Let us also remember Peter: three times he denied Jesus, precisely when he should have been closest to him. And when he hits rock bottom, he meets the gaze of Jesus who patiently, wordlessly, says to him, "Peter, don't be afraid of your weakness, trust in me." Peter understands, he feels the loving gaze of

Jesus, and he weeps. How beautiful is this gaze of Jesus—how much tenderness is there! Brothers and sisters, let us never lose trust in the patience and mercy of God!

Let us think too of the two disciples on the way to Emmaus: their sad faces, their barren journey, their despair. But Jesus does not abandon them: he walks beside them, and not only that! Patiently he explains the Scriptures, which spoke of him, and he stays to share a meal with them. This is God's way of doing things: he is

> *Let us remember this in our lives as Christians: God always waits for us, even when we have left him behind!*

not impatient like us, who often want everything all at once, even in our dealings with other people. God is patient with us because he loves us, and those who love are able to understand, to hope, and to inspire confidence. They do not give up, they do not burn bridges, they are able to forgive. Let us remember this in our lives as Christians: God always waits for us, even when we have left him behind! He is never far from us, and if we return to him, he is ready to embrace us.

I am always struck when I reread the parable of the merciful father; it impresses me because it always gives me great hope. Think of that younger son who was in the father's house, who was loved; and yet he wants his part of the inheritance. He goes off, spends everything, hits rock bottom, where he could not be more distant from the father. Yet when he is at his lowest, he misses the warmth of the father's house and he goes back. And the father? Had he forgotten the son? No, never. He is there, he sees the son from afar; he was waiting for him every hour of every day. The son was always in his father's heart, even though he had left him, even though he had squandered his whole inheritance, his freedom. The father, with patience, love, hope, and mercy had never for a second stopped thinking about him, and as soon as he sees him still far off, he runs out to meet him and embraces him with tenderness, the tenderness of God, without a word of reproach: his son has returned! And that is the joy of the father. In that embrace for his son is all this joy: he has returned! God is always waiting for us; he never grows tired. Jesus shows us this merciful patience of God so that we can regain confidence, hope—always! A great German theologian, Romano Guardini, said that God responds to our weakness by his patience, and this is the reason for our confidence, our hope (see *Glaubenserkenntnis* [Würzburg, 1949], p. 28). It is like a dialogue between our weakness and the patience of God; it is a dialogue that, if we have it, will grant us hope.

I would like to emphasize one other thing: God's patience has to call forth in us *the courage to return to him*, however many mistakes and sins there may be in our life. Jesus tells Thomas to put his hand in the wounds of his hands and his feet and in his side. We too can enter the wounds of Jesus; we can actually touch him. This happens every time we receive the sacraments with faith. St. Bernard, in a fine homily, said: "Through the wounds of Jesus I can suck honey from the rock and oil from the flinty rock (see Deut. 32:13), I can taste and see the goodness of the Lord" (*On the Song of Songs* 61:4). It is there, in the wounds of Jesus, that we are truly secure; there we encounter the boundless love of his heart. Thomas understood this. St. Bernard goes on to ask: But what can I count on? My own merits? No. "My merit is God's mercy. I am by no means lacking merits as long as he is rich in mercy. If the mercies of the Lord are manifold, I too will abound in merits" (61:5). This is important: the courage to trust in Jesus' mercy, to trust in his patience, to seek refuge always in the wounds of his love. St. Bernard even stated, "So what if my conscience gnaws at me for my many sins? 'Where sin has abounded, there grace has abounded all the more' (Rom. 5:20)" (61:5).

Maybe someone among us here is thinking, *My sin is so great, I am as far from God as the younger son in the parable; my unbelief is like that of Thomas. I don't have the courage to go back, to believe that God can welcome me and that he is waiting for me, of all people.* But God is indeed waiting for you; he asks of you only the courage to go to him.

> But God is indeed waiting for you; he asks of you only the courage to go to him.

How many times in my pastoral ministry have I heard it said, "Father, I have many sins"? And I have always pleaded, "Don't be afraid, go to him, he is waiting for you, he will take care of everything." We hear many offers from the world around us; but let us take up God's offer instead: his is a caress of love. For God, we are not numbers, we are

2

The Light of Faith

Lumen fidei, nos. 4 and 34, 29 June 2013

There is an urgent need, then, to see once again that faith is a light, and once the flame of faith dies out, all other lights begin to dim. The light of faith is unique, because it is capable of illuminating *every* aspect of human existence. A light this powerful cannot come from us but from a more primordial source: in a word, it must come from God. Faith is born of an encounter with the living God who calls us and reveals his love, a love that precedes us and upon which we can lean for security and for building our lives. Transformed by this love, we gain fresh vision, new eyes to see; we realize that it contains a great promise of fulfillment, and that a vision of the future opens up before us. Faith, received from God as a supernatural gift, becomes a light for our way, guiding our journey through time. It is a light coming from the past, the light of the foundational memory of the life of Jesus, which revealed his perfectly trustworthy love, a love capable of triumphing over death. Yet because Christ has risen and draws us beyond death, faith is also a light coming from the future and opening before us vast horizons that guide us beyond our isolated selves toward the breadth of communion. We come to see that faith does not dwell in shadow and gloom; it is a light for our darkness.

The light of love proper to faith can illumine the questions of our own time concerning truth. Truth nowadays is often reduced to the subjective authenticity of the individual, valid only to the life of the individual. A common truth intimidates us, for we identify it with the intransigent demands of totalitarian systems. But if truth is a truth of love, if it is a truth disclosed in personal encounter with the Other and with others, then it can be set free from its enclosure in individuals and become part of the common good. As a truth of love, it is not one that can be imposed by force; it is not a truth that stifles the individual. Since it is born of love, it can penetrate to the heart, to the personal core of each man and woman. Clearly, then, faith is not intransigent but grows in respectful coexistence with others. One who believes may not be presumptuous; on the contrary, truth leads to humility, because believers know that, rather than ourselves possessing truth, it is truth that embraces and possesses us. Far from making us inflexible, the security of faith sets us on a journey; it enables witness and dialogue with all.

> *The truth of love cannot be imposed by force; it is not a truth that stifles the individual.*

3

The Christian Message

Homily for the Easter Vigil, 30 March 2013

In the Gospel of the Easter Vigil, we first meet the women who go to the tomb of Jesus with spices to anoint his body (see Luke 24:1–3). They go to perform an act of compassion, a traditional act of affection and love for a dear departed person, just as we would. They had followed Jesus, they had listened to his words, they had felt understood by him in their dignity, and they had accompanied him to the very end, to Calvary and to the moment when he was taken down from the cross. We can imagine their feelings as they make their way to the tomb: a certain sadness, a sorrow that Jesus has left them, that he died, that his life has come to an end. Life will now go on as before. Yet the women continue to feel love, the love for Jesus that now leads them to his tomb.

But at this point, something completely new and unexpected happens, something that upsets their hearts and their plans, something that will upset their whole life. They see the stone removed from before the tomb; they draw near, and they do not find the Lord's body. It is an event that leaves them perplexed and hesitant, full of questions: "What happened?" "What is the meaning of all this?" (see Luke 24:4).

Doesn't the same thing happen to us when something completely new occurs in our everyday life? We stop short, we don't understand, we don't know what to do. *Newness* often makes us fearful, including the newness God brings us, the newness God asks of us. We are like the apostles in the Gospel:

often we would prefer to hold on to our own security, to stand in front of a tomb, to think about someone who has died, someone who ultimately lives on only as a memory, like the great historical figures from the past. We are afraid of God's surprises. Dear brothers and sisters, we are afraid of God's surprises! He always surprises us! The Lord is like that.

Brothers and sisters, let us not be closed to the newness that God wants to bring into our lives! Are we often weary, disheartened, and sad? Do we feel weighed down by our sins? Do we think that we won't be able to cope? Let us not close our hearts, let us not lose confidence, let us never give up. There are no situations that God cannot change; there is no sin that he cannot forgive if only we open ourselves to him.

But let us return to the Gospel, to the women, and take one step further. They find the tomb empty, the body of Jesus is not there, something new has happened, but all of this still doesn't tell them anything certain. It raises questions; it leaves them confused, without offering an answer. And suddenly there are two men in dazzling clothes who say, "Why do you look for the living among the dead? He is not here; but has risen" (Luke 24:5–6). What began as a simple act, done surely out of love—going to the tomb—has now turned into an event, a truly life-changing event. Nothing remains as it was before, not only in the lives of those women, but also in our own lives and in the history of humankind. Jesus is not dead, he has risen, he is alive! He does not simply return to life; rather, he is life itself, because he is the Son of God, *the living God* (see Num. 14:21–28; Deut. 5:26; Josh. 3:10).

Jesus no longer belongs to the past but lives in the present and is projected toward the future; Jesus is the everlasting "today" of God. This is how the newness of God appears to the women, the disciples, and all of us: as victory over sin, evil, and death—over everything that crushes life and makes it seem less human. And this is a message meant for me and for you, dear sister, for you, dear brother. How often does Love have to tell us, "Why do you look for the living among the dead?" Our daily problems and worries can wrap us up in ourselves, in sadness and bitterness . . . and that is where death is. That is not the place to look for the One who is alive!

Let the risen Jesus enter your life—welcome him as a friend, with trust: he is life! If up till now you have kept him at a distance, step forward. He will receive you with open arms. If you have been indifferent, take a risk; you won't be disappointed. If following him seems difficult,

> *If up till now you have kept Jesus at a distance, step forward. He will receive you with open arms.*

don't be afraid. Trust him, be confident that he is close to you, he is with you, and he will give you the peace you are looking for and the strength to live as he would have you do.

4

The Revolution of Freedom

Address to the Participants in the Ecclesial Convention of the Diocese of Rome, 17 June 2013

The apostle Paul ended one passage of his letter to the Romans with these words: "you are no longer under law but under grace" (Rom. 6:14). And this is our life: walking under grace, because the Lord has loved us, has saved us, has forgiven us. The Lord has done all things, and this is grace, God's grace. We are on our way under the grace of God who came down to us in Jesus Christ who saved us.

However, this opens us toward a wide horizon, and this is a joy to us. "You are not under law but under grace." What does this "living under grace" mean? It is our joy; it is our freedom. We are free. Why? Because we live under grace. We are no longer slaves of the Law; we are free, because Jesus Christ liberated us, he gave us freedom, the full freedom of God's children, in which we live under grace. This is a treasure. I shall try to explain something of this mystery, which is so beautiful and so important: living under grace.

Baptism, this admittance to being "under law," "under grace," is a revolution. There have been so many revolutionaries in history, many indeed. Yet none of them has had the force of this revolution that brought Jesus to us: a revolution to transform history, a revolution that changes the human heart in depth. The revolutions of history have changed political and economic systems, but none has really changed the human heart. True revolution, the revolution that radically transforms life, was brought about by Jesus Christ through his resurrection. Benedict XVI said of this revolution that "it is the greatest mutation in the history of humanity."

Let us think about this: it is the greatest mutation in humanity's history. It is a true revolution; we are revolutionaries and, what is more, revolutionaries of this revolution. For we have taken this road of the greatest metamorphosis in humanity's history. In this day and age, unless Christians are revolutionaries, they are not Christians. They must be revolutionaries

In this day and age, unless Christians are revolutionaries, they are not Christians. They must be revolutionaries through grace!

through grace! Grace itself, which the Father gives us through the crucified, dead, and risen Jesus Christ, makes us revolutionaries because—and once again I cite Benedict XVI—"he is the greatest mutation in the history of humanity" because he changes the heart.

The prophet Ezekiel said, "I will take out of your flesh the heart of stone and give you a heart of flesh." This is the experience the apostle Paul had after his encounter with Jesus on the road to Damascus. It radically changed his outlook on life, and he received baptism. God transformed his heart! However, only think: a persecutor, a man who hounded out the Church and Christians, a man who became a saint, a Christian to the marrow, a genuine Christian! First he was a violent persecutor, then he became an apostle, a witness of Jesus Christ so brave that he was not afraid of suffering martyrdom. In the end, the Saul who wanted to kill those who proclaimed the Gospel gave his own life to proclaim it.

This is the mutation, the most important mutation about which Pope Benedict spoke to us. He changes your heart, from that of a sinner—a sinner: we are all sinners—he transforms you into a saint. Is there any one of us who is not a sinner? If so, raise your hand! We are all sinners, each and every one. We are all sinners! But the grace of Jesus Christ saves us from sin: it saves us!

If we—all of us—accept the grace of Jesus Christ, he changes our heart and from sinners makes us saints. To become holy we do not need to turn our eyes away and look somewhere else, or have as it were the face on a holy card! No, no, that is not necessary. To become saints only one thing is necessary:

to accept the grace that the Father gives us in Jesus Christ. There, this grace changes our heart. We continue to be sinners for we are weak, but with this grace which makes us feel that the Lord is good, that the Lord is merciful, that the Lord waits for us, that the Lord pardons us—this immense grace that changes our heart.

5

Being with Christ

Address to the Participants at the International Congress on Catechesis, 27 September 2013

Now I am going to speak about three things: one, two, three, the way the old-fashioned Jesuits did . . . One, two, three!

First of all, to start anew from Christ means *being close to him*, being close to Jesus. Jesus stresses the importance of this with the disciples at the Last Supper, as he prepares to give us his own greatest gift of love, his sacrifice on the cross. Jesus uses the image of the vine and the branches and says, *Abide in my love, remain attached to me, as the branch is attached to the vine*. If we are joined to him, then we are able to bear fruit. This is what it means to be close to Christ. Abide in Jesus! This means remaining attached to him, in him, and with him, talking to him. Abide in Jesus!

The first thing for a disciple is to be with the Master, to listen to him and learn from him. This is always true, and it is true at every moment of our lives. I remember, in the diocese, the diocese I had first, how I would often see catechists finish their training courses and say, "I have the title of catechist!" This means nothing; you have nothing, you took a little journey. What good will it do you? But one thing is true. Being a catechist is not a title; it is an attitude of abiding with him, and it lasts for a lifetime! It means abiding in the Lord's presence and letting ourselves be led by him.

I ask you: How do you abide in the presence of the Lord? When you visit the Lord, when you look at the tabernacle, what do you do? Without speaking . . . "But I speak, I talk, I think, I meditate, I listen . . ." Very good! But do you let yourself be looked at by the Lord? [May we let] ourselves be gazed upon by the Lord. He looks at us, and this is itself a way of praying. Do you allow yourselves to be gazed upon by the Lord? But how do you do this? You look at the tabernacle and you let yourselves be looked at . . . it is simple! "It is a bit boring; I fall asleep." Fall asleep then, sleep! He is still looking at you. But know for sure that he is looking at you! This is much more important than having the title of catechist. It is part of "being" a catechist. This warms the heart, igniting the fire of friendship with the Lord, making you feel that he truly sees you, that he is close to you and loves you.

In one of my visits here in Rome, at a Mass, a fairly young man came up to me and said, "Father, it is nice to meet you, but I don't believe in anything! I don't have the gift of faith!" He understood that faith is a gift. "I don't have the gift of faith! What do you have to say to me?"

"Don't be discouraged," I said. "God loves you. Let yourself be gazed upon by him! Nothing else." And this is the same thing I would say to you: let yourselves be gazed at by the Lord! I understand that for you it is not so easy, especially for those who are married and have children, it is difficult to find a long period of quiet time. Yet, thanks be to God, it is not necessary for everyone to do this in the same way. In the Church, there are a variety of vocations and a variety of spiritualities. What is important is to find the way best suited for you to *be with the Lord*, and this everyone can do; it is possible for every state of life. Now each one of you could ask, how am I experiencing "being" with Jesus? This is a question I leave you: "How do I experience this remaining with Jesus, abiding in Jesus? Do I find time to remain in his presence, in silence, to be looked upon by him? Do I let his fire warm my heart?" If the warmth of God, of his love, of his tenderness, is not in our own hearts, then how can we, who are poor sinners, warm the heart of others? Think about it!

> *Do I find time to remain in his presence, in silence, to be looked upon by him? Do I let his fire warm my heart?*

The second element is this: starting anew with Christ means *imitating him by leaving ourselves behind and going out to encounter others.* This is a beautiful experience, and yet a paradox. Why? Because when we put Christ at the center of our life, we ourselves don't become the center! The more that you unite yourself to Christ and he becomes the center of your life, the more he leads you out of yourself, leads you from making yourself the center and opens you to others. This is the true dynamism of love; this is the movement of God himself! God is the center, but he is always self-gift, relationship, love that gives itself away . . . and this is what we will become if we remain united to Christ. He will draw us into this dynamism of love. Where there is true life in Christ, there follows an openness to others, and so a going out from oneself to encounter others in the name of Christ. And this is the job of the catechist: constantly to go forth to others out of love, to bear witness to Jesus and to talk about Jesus, to proclaim Jesus. This is important because the Lord does it; it is the Lord himself who impels us to go forth.

The heart of a catechist always beats with this systolic and diastolic movement: union with Christ, encounter with others. Both of these: I am one with Jesus, and I go forth to encounter others. If one of these movements is missing, the heart no longer beats; it can no longer live. The heart of the catechist receives the gift of the *kerygma* and in turn offers it to others as a gift. What a little word: *gift*! The catechist is conscious of having received a gift, the gift of faith, and he or she then gives that gift in turn to others. This is something beautiful. We don't keep a percentage for ourselves! Whatever we receive, we give! This is not commerce! It is not a business! It is pure gift: a gift received and a gift given. And the catechist is right there, at the center of this exchange of gifts. That is the nature itself of the *kerygma*: it is a gift that generates mission, that compels us to go beyond ourselves.

St. Paul says that "the love of Christ compels us," but this "compels us" can also be translated as "possesses us." And so it is: love attracts us and sends us; it draws us in and gives us to others. This tension marks the beating of the heart of the Christian, especially the heart of the catechist. Let us all ask ourselves, Is this what causes my heart to beat as a catechist, union with Christ and encounter with others? With this movement of systole and diastole? Are we being fed by our relationship with the Lord, so that we can bring him to others, and not keep it for ourselves? I'll tell you, I don't understand how a catechist can remain stationary, without this movement. I don't understand!

The third element is along these lines: starting anew with Christ means *not being afraid to go with him to the outskirts*. Here I think of the story of Jonah, a really interesting figure, especially for these times of great change and uncertainty. Jonah is a devout man, with a tranquil and ordered life, which causes him to have a clear-cut way of seeing things and to judge everything and everyone accordingly. He has it all figured out: this is the truth! He is rigid! So, when the Lord calls him and tells him to go and preach to Nineveh, the great pagan city, Jonah doesn't like it. "Go there? But I have the whole truth here!" He doesn't like it. Nineveh is outside his comfort zone; it is on the outskirts of his world. So he escapes, he sets off for Spain; he runs away and boards a ship that will take him there. Go and reread the book of Jonah! It is short, but it is a very instructive parable, especially for those of us in the Church.

What does all this teach us? It teaches us not to be afraid to pass beyond our comfort zone and to follow God, because God is always pushing, pressing forward. But do you know something? God is not afraid! Do you realize this? He isn't afraid. He is always bigger than our little way of seeing things! God is not afraid of the outskirts. If you go to the outskirts, you will find him there. God is always faithful and creative. But, really, is there such a thing as a catechist who is not creative? Creativity is what sustains us as catechists. God is creative; he is not closed, and so he is never inflexible. God is not rigid! He welcomes us, he meets us, he understands us.

To be faithful, to be creative, we need to be able to change. To change! And why must I change? So that I can adapt to the situations in which I must proclaim the Gospel. To stay close to God, we need to know how to set out; we must not be afraid to set out. If a catechist gives in to fear, then he or she is a coward. If a catechist has an easy time of it, he or she will end up being a statue in a museum. We have a lot of these! Please, no more statues in the museum! If a catechist is rigid, he or she will dry up and wither. I ask you: Do any of you want to be a coward, a statue in a museum, dried up and withered? Is that what you want to be? [The catechists reply, "No!"] No? Are you sure? Good! I am now going to say something I have already said many times before, but it comes from the heart.

Whenever we Christians are enclosed in our groups, our movements, our parishes, in our little worlds, we remain closed, and the same thing happens to us that happens to anything closed: when a room is closed, it begins to get dank. If a

> *I would prefer a thousand times over a bruised Church to an ill Church!*

person is closed up in that room, he or she becomes ill! Whenever Christians are enclosed in their groups, parishes, and movements, they take ill. If a Christian goes to the streets, or to the outskirts, he or she may risk the same thing that can happen to anyone out there: an accident. How often have we seen accidents on the road! But I am telling you: I would prefer a thousand times over a bruised Church to an ill Church! A Church, a catechist, with the courage to risk going out, and not a catechist who is studious, who knows everything but is always closed—such a person is not well. And sometimes he or she is not well in the head . . .

But, careful! Jesus does not say, *Go off and do things on your own*. No! That is not what he is saying. Jesus says, *Go, for I am with you!* This is what is so beautiful for us; it is what guides us. If we go out to bring his Gospel with love, with a true apostolic spirit, with parrhesia, he walks with us, he goes ahead of us, and he gets there first. As we say in Spanish, *nos primerea*. By now you know what I mean by this. It is the same thing that the Bible tells us. In the Bible, the Lord says: *I am like the flower of the almond*. Why? Because that is the first flower to blossom in the spring. He is always the first! This is fundamental for us: God is always ahead of us! When we think about going far away, to an extreme outskirt, we may be a bit afraid, but in fact God is already there. Jesus is waiting for us in the hearts of our brothers and sisters, in their wounded bodies, in their hardships, in their lack of faith. But can I tell you about one of the "outskirts" which breaks my heart? I saw it in my first diocese. It is children who don't even know how to make the sign of the cross. In Buenos Aires there are many children who can't make the sign of the cross. This is one of the "outskirts"! And Jesus is there, waiting for you to help that child make the sign of the cross. He's always there first.

Dear catechists, I have made my three points. Always start anew from Christ! I thank you for everything that you do, but above all, because you are part of the Church, the pilgrim People of God, and you accompany God's people on that pilgrimage. Let us remain with Christ—abiding in Christ—and let us always try to be one with him. Let us follow him; let us imitate him in his movement of love, in his going forth to meet humanity. Let us go forth and open doors. Let us have the audacity to mark out new paths for proclaiming the Gospel.

PART TWO

A Poor Church for the Poor

6

Listen to the Cry of the Poor

Evangelii gaudium, nos. 186–88, 198, 24 November 2013

Our faith in Christ, who became poor, and was always close to the poor and the outcast, is the basis of our concern for the integral development of society's most neglected members.

Each individual Christian and every community is called to be an instrument of God for the liberation and promotion of the poor, and for enabling them to be fully a part of society. This demands that we be docile and attentive to the cry of the poor and come to their aid. A mere glance at the Scriptures is enough to make us see how our gracious Father wants to hear the cry of the poor: "I have observed the misery of my people who are in Egypt; I have heard their cry on account of their taskmasters. Indeed, I know their sufferings, and I have come down to deliver them . . . so I will send you" (Exod. 3:7–8, 10). We also see how he is concerned for their needs: "When the Israelites cried out to the Lord, the Lord raised up for them a deliverer" (Judg. 3:15). If we, who are God's means of hearing the poor, turn deaf ears to this plea, we oppose the Father's will and his plan; that poor person "might cry to the Lord against you, and you would incur guilt" (Deut. 15:9). A lack of solidarity toward his or her needs will directly affect our relationship with God: "For if in bitterness of soul he calls down a curse upon you, his Creator will hear his prayer" (Sir. 4:6). The old question always returns: "How does God's love abide in anyone who has the world's goods, and sees a brother or sister in need and yet refuses help?" (1 John 3:17). Let us recall also how bluntly the apostle James speaks of the cry of the oppressed: "The wages of the laborers who mowed your fields, which you kept back by fraud, cry out, and the cries of the harvesters have reached the ears of the Lord of hosts" (James 5:4).

The Church has realized that the need to heed this plea is itself born of the liberating action of grace within each of us, and thus it is not a question of a mission reserved only for a few: "The Church, guided by the Gospel of mercy and by love for humankind, *hears the cry for justice* and intends to respond to it with all her might." In this context we can understand Jesus' command to his disciples: "You yourselves give them something to eat!" (Mark 6:37). This means working to eliminate the structural causes of poverty and to promote the integral development of the poor, as well as small daily acts of solidarity in meeting the real needs we encounter. The word *solidarity* is a little worn and at times poorly understood, but it refers to something more than a few sporadic acts of generosity. It presumes the creation of a new mind-set that thinks in terms of community and the priority of the life of all over the appropriation of goods by a few.

For the Church, the option for the poor is primarily a theological category rather than a cultural, sociological, political, or philosophical one. God shows the poor "his first mercy." This divine preference has consequences for the faith life of all Christians, because we are called to

> We need to let ourselves be evangelized by the poor. They have much to teach us.

have "this mind . . . which was in Jesus Christ" (Phil. 2:5). Inspired by this, the Church has made an *option for the poor*, which is understood as a "special form of primacy in the exercise of Christian charity, to which the whole tradition of the Church bears witness." This option—as Benedict XVI has taught—"is implicit in our Christian faith in a God who became poor for us, so as to enrich us with his poverty." This is why I want a Church that is poor and for the poor. They have much to teach us. Not only do they share in the *sensus fidei*, but in their difficulties they know the suffering Christ. We need to let ourselves be evangelized by them. The new evangelization is an invitation to acknowledge the saving power at work in their lives and to put them at the center of the Church's pilgrim way. We are called to find Christ in them, to lend our voice to their causes, but also to be their friends, to listen to them, to speak for them, and to embrace the mysterious wisdom that God wishes to share with us through them.

7

A House of Communion

General Audience, 25 November 2013

In the Creed we say, "I believe in one . . . Church." In other words, we profess that the Church is one, and this Church by her nature is one. However, if we look at the Catholic Church in the world, we discover that it includes almost three thousand dioceses scattered over all the continents: so many languages, so many cultures! Present here are many bishops from many diverse cultures, from many countries. There is a bishop of Sri Lanka, a bishop of South Africa, a bishop from India, there are many here . . . bishops from Latin America. The Church is spread throughout the world! And yet the thousands of Catholic communities form a unit. How can this be?

We find a concise answer in the *Compendium of the Catechism of the Catholic Church*, which says: the Catholic Church in the world "has but one faith, one sacramental life, one apostolic succession, one common hope, and one and the same charity" (no. 161). It is a beautiful definition—clear, it orients us well. Unity in faith, hope, and charity, unity in the sacraments, in the ministry; these are like the pillars that hold up the one great edifice of the Church. Wherever we go, even to the smallest parish in the most remote corner of this earth, there is the one Church. We are at home, we are in the family, and we are among brothers and sisters. And this is a great gift of God! The Church is one for us all. There is not one Church for Europeans, one for Africans, one for Americans, one for Asians, and one for those who live in Oceania. No, she is one and the same everywhere. It is like being in a family:

some of its members may be far away, scattered across the world, but the deep bonds that unite all the members of a family stay solid however great the distance.

I am thinking, for example, of my experience of World Youth Day in Rio de Janeiro. In that endless crowd of young people on the beach at Copacabana we could hear many languages spoken, we could note very different facial features, and we came across different cultures. Yet there was profound unity—they formed one Church, they were united, and one could sense it. Let us all ask ourselves: As a Catholic, do I feel this unity? As a Catholic, do I live this unity of the Church? Or does it not concern me because I am closed within my own small group or within myself? Am I one of those who "privatize" the Church to their own group, their own country or their own friends? It is sad to find a privatized Church out of selfishness or a lack of faith. It is sad! When I hear that so many Christians in the world are suffering, am I indifferent, or is it as if one of my family were suffering? When I think or hear it said that many Christians are persecuted and give their lives for their faith, does this touch my heart or not? Am I open to a brother or sister of the family who is giving his or her life for Jesus Christ? Do we pray for each other? I have a question for you, but don't answer out loud, only in your heart. How many of you pray for Christians who are being persecuted? How many? Everyone respond in your heart. Do I pray for my brother, for my sister who is in difficulty because they confess and defend their faith? It is important to look beyond our own boundaries, to feel that we are Church, one family in God!

Let us go a step further and ask ourselves: Are there wounds in this unity? Can we hurt this unity? Unfortunately, we see that in the process of history, and now too, we do not always live in unity. At times misunderstanding arises, as well as conflict, tension, and division, which injure the Church, and so she does not have the face we should like her to have; she does not express love, the love that God desires. It is we who create wounds! And if we look at the divisions that still exist among Christians, Catholics, Orthodox, Protestants . . . we are aware of the effort required to make this unity fully visible. God gives us unity, but we often have a lot of trouble putting it into practice. It is necessary to seek to build communion, to teach communion, to get the better of misunderstandings and divisions, starting with the family, with ecclesial reality, in ecumenical dialogue too. Our world needs unity; this is an age in which we all need unity. We need reconciliation and communion, and the Church is the home of communion.

St. Paul told the Christians of Ephesus, "I therefore, a prisoner for the Lord, beg you to lead a life worthy of the calling to which you have been called, with all lowliness and meekness, with patience, forbearing one another in love, eager to maintain the unity of the Spirit in the bond of peace" (Eph. 4:1–3). Humility, meekness, magnanimity, and love to preserve unity! These, these are the roads, the true roads of the Church. Let us listen to this again. Humility against vanity, against arrogance—humility, meekness, magnanimity, and love preserve unity. Then Paul continued: there is one body, that of Christ, that we receive in the Eucharist; and one Spirit, the Holy Spirit, who enlivens and constantly re-creates the Church; one hope, eternal life; one single faith, one baptism, one God and Father of us all (see Eph. 4:4–6). The wealth of what unites us! This is the true wealth: what unites us, not what divides us. This is the wealth of the Church! Let each one ask him- or herself today, "Do I increase harmony in my family, in my parish, in my community, or am I a gossip? Am I a cause of division or embarrassment?" And you know the harm that gossiping does to the Church, to the parishes, the communities. Gossip does harm! Gossip wounds. Before Christians open their mouths to gossip, they should bite their tongue! To bite one's tongue: this does us good because the tongue swells and can no longer speak, cannot gossip. "Am I humble enough to patiently stitch up, through sacrifice, the open wounds in communion?"

Finally, the last step, which takes us to a greater depth. Now, this is a good question: who is the driving force of the Church's unity? It is the Holy Spirit, whom we have all received at

The Holy Spirit is the mover. This is why prayer is important.

baptism and also in the sacrament of confirmation. It is the Holy Spirit. Our unity is not primarily a fruit of our own consensus or of the democracy in the Church, or of our effort to get along with one another; rather, it comes from the One who creates unity in diversity, because the Holy Spirit is harmony and always creates harmony in the Church. And harmonious unity in the many different cultures, languages, and ways of thinking. The Holy Spirit is the mover. This is why prayer is important. It is the soul of our commitment as men and women of communion, of unity. Pray to the Holy Spirit that he may come and create unity in the Church.

Let us ask the Lord: Lord, grant that we be more and more united, never to be instruments of division. Enable us to commit ourselves, as the beautiful Franciscan prayer says, to sowing love where there is hatred; where there is injury, pardon; and union where there is discord.

8

A House That Welcomes All

General Audience, 2 October 2013

In the Creed, after professing "I believe in one Church," we add the adjective *holy*; we affirm the sanctity of the Church, and this is a characteristic that has been present from the beginning in the consciousness of early Christians, who were simply called "the holy people" (see Acts 9:13, 32, 41; Rom. 8:27; 1 Cor. 6:1), because they were certain that it is the action of God, the Holy Spirit, that sanctifies the Church.

But in what sense is the Church holy if we see that the historical Church, on her long journey through the centuries, has had so many difficulties, problems, dark moments? How can a Church consisting of human beings, of sinners, be holy? Sinful men, sinful women, sinful priests, sinful sisters, sinful bishops, sinful cardinals, a sinful pope? Everyone. How can such a Church be holy?

To respond to this question, I would like to be led by a passage from the letter of St. Paul to the Christians of Ephesus. The apostle, taking as an example family relationships, states that "Christ loved the Church and gave himself up for her, that he might sanctify her" (Eph. 5:25–26). Christ loved the Church, by giving himself on the cross. And this means that the Church is holy because she comes from God, who is holy; he is faithful to her and does not abandon her to the power of death and of evil (see Matt. 16:18). She is holy because Jesus Christ, the Holy One of God (cf. Mark 1:24), is indissolubly united to her (see Matt. 28:20); she is holy because she is guided by the

30

Holy Spirit who purifies, transforms, and renews. She is not holy by her own merits but because God makes her holy; it is the fruit of the Holy Spirit and of his gifts. It is not we who make her holy. It is God, the Holy Spirit, who in his love makes the Church holy.

You could say to me, "But the Church is made up of sinners; we see them every day." And this is true: we are a Church of sinners. And we sinners are called to let ourselves be transformed, renewed, sanctified by God. Throughout history, some have been tempted to say that the Church is the Church of only the pure and the perfectly consistent, and it expels all the rest. This is not true! This is heresy! The Church, which is holy, does not reject sinners; she does not reject us all; she does not reject us because she calls everyone, welcomes them, is open even to those furthest from her; she calls everyone to allow themselves to be enfolded by the mercy, the tenderness, and the forgiveness of the Father, who offers everyone the possibility of meeting him, of journeying toward sanctity.

"Well! Father, I am a sinner; I have tremendous sins. How can I possibly feel part of the Church?" Dear brother, dear sister, this is exactly what the Lord wants, that you say to him, "Lord, here I am, with my sins." Is one of you here without sin? Anyone? No one, not one of us. We all carry our sins with us. But the Lord wants to hear us say to him, "Forgive me, help me to walk, change my heart!" And the Lord can change your heart. In the Church, the God we encounter is not a merciless judge but is like the Father in the Gospel parable. You may be like the son who left home, who sank to the depths, farthest from the Gospel. When you have the strength to say, "I want to come home," you will find the door open. God will come to meet you because he is always waiting for you—God is always waiting for you. God embraces you, kisses you, and celebrates. That is how the Lord is, that is how the tenderness of our heavenly Father is. The Lord wants us to belong to a Church that knows how to open her arms and welcome everyone, that is not a house for the few, but a house for everyone, where all can be renewed, transformed, sanctified by his love—the strongest and the weakest, sinners, the indifferent, those who feel discouraged or lost.

The Church offers all the possibility of following a path of holiness, which is the path of the Christian; she brings us to encounter Jesus Christ in the sacraments, especially in confession and in the Eucharist; she communicates the Word of God to us, she lets us live in charity, in the love of God for all. Let us ask ourselves, then, Will we let ourselves be sanctified? Are we a Church that calls and welcomes sinners with open arms, that gives courage and hope, or are we a Church closed in on herself?

Are we a Church that calls and welcomes sinners with open arms, that gives courage and hope, or are we a Church closed in on herself?

a Church that calls and welcomes sinners with open arms, that gives courage and hope, or are we a Church closed in on herself? Are we a Church where the love of God dwells, where one cares for the other, where one prays for the other?

A final question: what can I, a weak fragile sinner, do? God says to you, *Do not be afraid of holiness; do not be afraid to aim high, to let yourself be loved and purified by God; do not be afraid to let yourself be guided by the Holy Spirit.* Let us be infected by the holiness of God. Every Christian is called to sanctity (see Dogmatic Constitution, *Lumen gentium*, nos. 19–42); and sanctity does not consist especially in doing extraordinary things, but in allowing God to act. It is the meeting of our weakness with the strength of his grace, it is having faith in his action that allows us to live in charity, to do everything with joy and humility, for the glory of God and as a service to our neighbor. There is a celebrated saying by the French writer Léon Bloy, who in the last moments of his life said, "The only real sadness in life is not becoming a saint." Let us not lose the hope of holiness; let us follow this path. Do we want to be saints? The Lord awaits us, with open arms; he waits to accompany us on the path to sanctity. Let us live in the joy of our faith, let us allow ourselves to be loved by the Lord . . . let us ask for this gift from God in prayer, for ourselves, and for others.

9

A House of Harmony

General Audience, 9 October 2013

"I believe in one, holy, catholic . . . Church." Today we pause to reflect on this mark of the Church: we say she is catholic, it is the Year of Catholicity. First of all, what does *catholic* mean? It comes from the Greek *kath' olon*, which means "according to the whole," the totality. In what sense does this totality apply to the Church? In what sense do we say the Church is catholic? I would say there are three basic meanings.

First, the Church is catholic because she is the space, the home in which *the faith* is proclaimed to us *in its entirety*, in which the salvation brought to us by Christ is offered to everyone. The Church enables us to encounter the mercy of God, which transforms us, for in her Jesus Christ is present who has given her the true confession of faith, the fullness of the sacramental life, and the authenticity of the ordained ministry. In the Church each one of us finds what is needed to believe, to live as Christians, to become holy, and to journey to every place and through every age.

To give an example, we can say that it is like family life. In the family, everything that enables us to grow, to mature, and to live is given to each of us. We cannot grow up by ourselves, we cannot journey on our own, in isolation; rather, we journey and grow in a community, in a family. And so it is in the Church! In the Church we can listen to the Word of God with the assurance that it is the message that the Lord has given us; in the Church we can encounter the Lord in the sacraments, which are the open windows through which the light of God is given to us, streams from which we can draw God's very life; in the Church we learn to live in the communion and love that come from God. Each one of us can ask himself or herself today: How do I live in the Church? When I go to church, is it as though I were at the stadium, at a football match? Is it as though I were at the cinema? No, it is something else. How do I go to church? How do I receive the gifts that the Church offers me to grow and mature as a Christian? Do I participate in the life of the community, or do I go to church and withdraw into my own problems, isolating myself from others? In this first sense, the Church is catholic because she is everyone's home. Everyone is a child of the Church, and in her all find their home.

A second meaning: the Church is catholic because she is *universal:* she is spread abroad through every part of the world, and she proclaims the Gospel to every man and to every woman. The Church is not a group of the elite; she does not concern only the few. The Church has no limits; she is sent to the totality of people, to the totality of the human race. And the one Church is present even in her smallest parts. Everyone can say: in my parish the Catholic Church is present, because it too is part of the

> *The Church does not rest solely beneath the shadow of our steeple; rather, she embraces a vast number of peoples and nations who profess the same faith, are nourished by the same Eucharist, and are served by the same pastors.*

universal Church, since it too contains the fullness of Christ's gifts: the faith, the sacraments, the (ordained) ministry. It is in communion with the bishop, with the pope, and it is open to everyone without distinction. The Church does not rest solely beneath the shadow of our steeple; rather, she embraces a vast number of peoples and nations who profess the same faith, are nourished by the same Eucharist, and are served by the same pastors. To feel that we are in communion with the whole Church, with all of the Catholic communities of the world great and small—this is beautiful! And then, to feel we are all on a mission, great and small communities alike, that we all must open our doors and go out for the sake of the Gospel. Let us ask ourselves, then, what do I do in order to communicate to others the joy of encountering the Lord, the joy of belonging to the Church? Proclaiming and bearing witness to the faith is not the work of the few; it also concerns me, you, each one of us!

A third and final thought: the Church is catholic because she is the "home of harmony," where *unity and diversity* know how to merge in order to become a great source of wealth. Let us think about the image of a symphony, which implies accord, harmony, various instruments playing together. Each one preserves its own unmistakable timbre, and the sounds characteristic of each blend together around a common theme. Then there is the one who directs it, the conductor, and as the symphony is performed all play together in harmony, but the timbre of each individual instrument is never eliminated; indeed, the uniqueness of each is greatly enhanced!

This is a beautiful image illustrating that the Church is like a great orchestra in which there is great variety. We are not all the same, and we do not all have to be the same. We are all different, varied, each of us with our own special qualities. And this is the beauty of the Church: everyone brings their own gifts, which God has given, for the sake of enriching others. And between the various components there is diversity; however, it is a diversity that does not enter into conflict and opposition. It is a variety that allows the Holy Spirit to blend it into harmony. He is the true "Maestro." He is harmony. And here let us ask ourselves: In our communities do we live in harmony or do we argue among ourselves? In my parish community, in my movement, in the place where I am part of the Church, is there gossip? If there is gossip, there is no harmony but rather conflict. And this is not the Church. The Church is everyone in harmony—never gossip about others, never argue! Let us accept others; let us accept that there is a fitting variety, that this person is different, that this person thinks about things in this way or that—that within one and the same faith we can think about things differently. Or do we tend to make everything uniform? But uniformity kills life. The life of the Church is variety, and when we want to impose this uniformity on everyone, we kill the gifts of the Holy Spirit.

Let us pray to the Holy Spirit, who is truly the author of this unity in variety, of this harmony, that he might make us ever more "catholic" in this Church that is catholic and universal!

10

Sent to Bring the Gospel to All the World

General Audience, 16 October 2013

When we recite the Creed, we say, "I believe in one, holy, catholic and apostolic Church." I don't know if you have ever reflected on the meaning of the expression "the Church is apostolic." Perhaps from time to time, coming to Rome, you have thought about the importance of the apostles Peter and Paul, who here gave their lives to bring and bear witness to the Gospel.

But it is even more. To profess that the Church is apostolic means to stress the constitutive bond that she has with the apostles, with that small group of twelve men whom Jesus one day called to himself; he called them by name, that they might remain with him and that he might send them out to preach (see Mark 3:13–19). *Apostle*, in fact, is a Greek word meaning "sent," "dispatched." An apostle is a person who has been given a mandate, sent to do something, and the apostles were chosen, called and sent out by Jesus to continue his work, that is, to pray—which is the primary job of an apostle—and, second, to proclaim the Gospel.

This is important, because when we think of the apostles, we might think that they were sent out only to proclaim the Gospel, to do many good deeds. However, a problem arose in the early times of the Church because of how much the apostles had to do, and that is why they instituted deacons, so that there would be more time for the apostles to pray and proclaim the Word of God. When we think of the successors of the apostles, the bishops—this includes the pope, for he too is a bishop—we must ask ourselves if this successor of the apostles prays first and then proclaims the Gospel: this is what it means to be an apostle, and this is what makes the Church apostolic. Every one of us, if we want to be apostles, as I shall explain now, must ask ourselves: Do I pray for the salvation of the world? Do I proclaim the Gospel? This is the Church apostolic! It is the constitutive bond that we have with the apostles.

Starting from this, I would like to focus briefly on the three meanings of the adjective *apostolic* as it is applied to the Church.

1. The Church is apostolic because she is *founded on the preaching and prayer of the apostles*, on the authority that was entrusted to them by Christ himself. St. Paul writes to the Christians of Ephesus: "You are no longer strangers and sojourners, but you are fellow citizens with the saints and members of the household of God, built upon the foundation of the apostles and prophets, Christ Jesus himself being a cornerstone" (Eph. 2:19–20); that is, he compares Christians to living stones that form an edifice that is the Church, and this edifice is founded on the apostles, who are like columns, and the cornerstone that carries it all is Jesus himself. Without Jesus the Church cannot exist! Jesus is the foundation of the Church—the foundation! The apostles lived with Jesus, they listened to his words, they shared his life; above all they were witnesses of his death and resurrection. Our faith, the Church that Christ willed, is not based on an idea; it is not based on a philosophy. It is based on Christ himself. And the Church is like a plant that over the long centuries has grown, has developed, has borne fruit, yet her roots are planted firmly in Christ and that fundamental experience of Christ which the apostles had, chosen and sent out by Jesus, reaching all the way to us. From this little plant to our day, this is how the Church has spread everywhere in the world.

2. But let us ask ourselves: How is it possible for us to be connected to that testimony? How could what the apostles' experienced with Jesus, what they heard from him, reach us? This is the second meaning of the term *apostolic*. The

> *This is the beauty of the Church: the presence of Jesus Christ among us.*

Catechism of the Catholic Church states that the Church is apostolic because "with the help of the Spirit dwelling in her, the Church *keeps and hands on* the teaching, the 'good deposit,' the salutary words she has heard from the Apostles" (no. 857). Over the centuries, the Church conserves this precious treasure, which is sacred Scripture, doctrine, the sacraments, the ministry of pastors, so that we can be faithful to Christ and share in his very life. It is like a river coursing through history, developing, irrigating; but running water always comes from a source, and the source is Christ himself: he is the Risen One, he is the Living One, and his words never pass away, for he does not pass: he is alive, he is among us today, he hears us and we speak to him, and he listens; he is in our hearts. Jesus is with us today! This is the beauty of the Church: the presence of Jesus Christ among us. Do we ever think about how important this gift that Jesus gave us is, the gift of the Church, where we can meet him? Do we ever think about how it is precisely the Church on her journey through the centuries—despite the difficulties, the problems, the weaknesses, our sins—that transmits to us the authentic message of Christ? That she gives us the certainty that what we believe in is really what Christ communicated to us?

3. My final thought: the Church is apostolic because she *is sent to bring the Gospel to all the world*. She continues in history the mission that Jesus entrusted to the apostles: "Go therefore and make disciples of all nations, baptizing them in the name of the Father and of the Son and of the Holy Spirit, teaching them to observe all that I have commanded you; and lo, I am with you always, to the close of the age" (Matt. 28:19–20). This is what Jesus told us to do! I insist on this missionary aspect, because Christ invites all to "go out" and encounter others; he sends us, he asks us to move in order to spread the joy of the Gospel! Once again let us ask ourselves: Are we missionaries by our words, and especially by our Christian life, by our witness? Or are we Christians closed in our hearts and in our churches—sacristy Christians? Are we Christians in name only, who live like pagans? We must ask ourselves these questions, which are not a rebuke. I ask myself as well: What kind of Christian am I? Is my witness true?

The Church's roots are in the teaching of the apostles, the authentic witnesses of Christ, but she looks to the future, she has the firm consciousness of being sent—sent by Jesus—of being missionary, bearing the name of Jesus by her prayer, proclaiming it and testifying to it. A Church that is closed in on herself and in the past, a Church that only sees the little rules of behavior, of attitude, is a Church that betrays her own identity; a closed Church betrays her own identity! Then, let us rediscover today all the beauty and responsibility of being the Church apostolic! And remember this: the Church is apostolic because we pray—our first duty—and because we proclaim the Gospel by our life and by our words.

PART THREE

Listening to the Spirit

11

Be Guided by the Holy Spirit

General Audience, 15 May 2013

Now I would like to reflect on the Holy Spirit's action in guiding the Church and each one of us to the Truth. Jesus himself told his disciples that the Holy Spirit "will guide you into all the truth" (John 16:13), since he himself is "the Spirit of Truth" (see John 14:17, 15:26, 16:13).

We are living in an age in which people are rather skeptical of truth. Benedict XVI has frequently spoken of relativism, that is, of the tendency to consider nothing definitive and to think that truth comes from consensus or from something we like. The question arises: Does *the* truth really exist? What is *the* truth? Can we know it? Can we find it? Here springs to my mind the question of Pontius Pilate, the Roman procurator, when Jesus reveals to him the deep meaning of his mission: "What is truth?" (John 18:37, 38). Pilate cannot understand that the truth is standing in front of him; he cannot see in Jesus the face of the truth that is the face of God. And yet Jesus is exactly this: the Truth that, in the fullness of time, "became flesh" (see John 1:1, 14) and came to dwell among us so that we might know it. The truth is not grasped as a thing; the truth is encountered. It is not a possession; it is an encounter with a Person.

> *The truth is not a possession; it is an encounter with a Person.*

But who can enable us to recognize that Jesus is the Word of Truth, the only begotten Son of God the Father? St. Paul teaches that "no one can say

43

'Jesus is Lord' except by the Holy Spirit" (1 Cor. 12:3). It is the Holy Spirit himself, the gift of the risen Christ, who makes us recognize the Truth. Jesus describes him as the "Paraclete," namely, "the one who comes to our aid," who is beside us to sustain us on this journey of knowledge. And at the Last Supper, Jesus assures the disciples that the Holy Spirit will teach them all things and remind them of all he has said to them (see John 14:26).

So how does the Holy Spirit act in our life and in the life of the Church in order to guide us to the Truth? First of all, he recalls and impresses in the hearts of believers the words Jesus spoke and, through these very words, the law of God—as the prophets of the Old Testament had foretold—is engraved in our hearts and becomes within us a criterion for evaluation in decisions and for guidance in our daily actions; it becomes a principle to live by. Ezekiel's great prophecy is brought about: "You shall be clean from all your uncleannesses, and from all your idols I will cleanse you. A new heart I will give you, and a new spirit I will put within you. . . . And I will put my spirit within you, and cause you to walk in my statutes and be careful to observe my ordinances" (Ezek. 36:25–27). Indeed, it is in our inmost depths that our actions come into being; it is the heart itself that must be converted to God, and the Holy Spirit transforms it when we open ourselves to him.

Then, as Jesus promised, the Holy Spirit guides us "into all the truth" (John 16:13); not only does he guide us to the encounter with Jesus, the fullness of the Truth, but he also guides us "into" the Truth—that is, he makes us enter into an ever-deeper communion with Jesus, giving us knowledge of all the things of God. And we cannot achieve this by our own efforts. Unless God enlightens us from within, our Christian existence will be superficial. The Church's tradition asserts that the Spirit of truth acts in our heart, inspiring that "sense of the faith" (*sensus fidei*) through which, as the Second Vatican Council states, the People of God, under the guidance of the magisterium, adheres unfailingly to the faith transmitted, penetrates it more deeply with the right judgment, and applies it more fully in life (see Dogmatic Constitution, *Lumen gentium*, no. 12). Let us try asking ourselves: Am I open to the action of the Holy Spirit? Do I pray to him to give me illumination, to make me more sensitive to God's things? This is a prayer we must pray every day: "Holy Spirit, make my heart open to the word of God, make my heart open to goodness, make my heart open to the beauty of God every day." I would like to ask everyone a question: how many of you pray every day to the Holy Spirit? There will not be many, but we must fulfill Jesus' wish and pray every day to the Holy Spirit that he open our heart to Jesus.

Let us think of Mary, who "kept all these things, pondering them in her heart" (Luke 2:19, 51). Acceptance of the words and truth of faith so that they may become life is brought about and increases under the action of the Holy Spirit. In this regard we must learn from Mary, we must relive her "yes," her unreserved readiness to receive the Son of God in her life, which was transformed from that moment. Through the Holy Spirit, the Father and the Son take up their abode with us: we live in God and of God. Yet is our life truly inspired by God? How many things do I put before God?

Dear brothers and sisters, we need to let ourselves be bathed in the light of the Holy Spirit so that he may lead us into the Truth of God, who is the one Lord of our life. In this Year of Faith let us ask ourselves whether we really have taken some steps to know Christ and the truth of faith better by reading and meditating on sacred Scripture, by studying the *Catechism*, and by receiving the sacraments regularly. However, let us ask ourselves at the same time what steps we are taking to ensure that faith governs the whole of our existence. We are not Christian "part-time," only at certain moments, in certain circumstances, in certain decisions; no one can be Christian in this way. We are Christian all the time! Totally! May Christ's truth, which the Holy Spirit teaches us and gives to us, always and totally affect our daily life. Let us call on him more often so that he may guide us on the path of disciples of Christ. Let us call on him every day. I am making this suggestion to you: let us invoke the Holy Spirit every day; in this way the Holy Spirit will bring us close to Jesus Christ.

12

Good News, Harmony, Mission

Homily on the Solemnity of Pentecost, 19 May 2013

On Pentecost Day we contemplate and relive in the liturgy the outpouring of the Holy Spirit sent by the risen Christ upon his Church, an event of grace that filled the Upper Room in Jerusalem and then spread throughout the world.

But what happened on that day, so distant from us and yet so close as to touch the very depths of our hearts? Luke gives us the answer in the passage of the Acts of the Apostles (Acts 2:1–11). The evangelist brings us back to Jerusalem, to the Upper Room, where the apostles were gathered. The first element that draws our attention is the sound that suddenly came from heaven "like the rush of a violent wind" and filled the house; then the "tongues as of fire" that divided and came to rest on each of the apostles. Sound and tongues of fire: these are clear, concrete signs that touch the apostles not only from without but also within, deep in their minds and hearts. As a result, "all of them were filled with the Holy Spirit," who unleashed his irresistible power with amazing consequences: they all "began to speak in different languages, as the Spirit gave them ability." A completely unexpected scene opens up before our eyes: a great crowd gathers, astonished because each one heard the apostles speaking in their own language. They all experience something new, something which had never happened before: "We hear them, each of us, speaking our own language." And what is it that they are speaking about? "God's deeds of power."

In the light of this passage from Acts, I would like to reflect on three words linked to the working of the Holy Spirit: *newness, harmony,* and *mission.*

1. *Newness* always makes us a bit fearful, because we feel more secure if we have everything under control, if we are the ones who build, program, and plan our lives in accordance

> Let us ask ourselves today: are we open to "God's surprises"?

with our own ideas, our own comfort, and our own preferences. This is also the case when it comes to God. Often we follow him, we accept him, but only up to a certain point. It is hard to abandon ourselves to him with complete trust, allowing the Holy Spirit to be the soul and guide of our lives in our every decision. We fear that God may force us to strike out on new paths and leave behind our all too narrow, closed, and selfish horizons in order to become open to his own. Yet throughout the history of salvation, whenever God reveals himself, he brings newness—God always brings newness—and demands our complete trust: Noah, mocked by all, builds an ark and is saved; Abram leaves his land with only a promise in hand; Moses stands up to the might of Pharaoh and leads his people to freedom; the apostles, huddled fearfully in the Upper Room, go forth with courage to proclaim the Gospel. This is not a question of novelty for novelty's sake, the search for something new to relieve our boredom, as is so often the case in our own day. The newness that God brings into our life is something that actually brings fulfillment, that gives true joy, true serenity, because God loves us and desires only our good. Let us ask ourselves today: are we open to "God's surprises"? Or are we closed and fearful before the newness of the Holy Spirit? Do we have the courage to strike out along the new paths that God's newness sets before us, or do we resist, barricaded in transient structures that have lost their capacity for openness to what is new? We would do well to ask ourselves these questions all through the day.

2. A second thought: the Holy Spirit would appear to create disorder in the Church, because he brings the diversity of charisms and gifts; yet all this, by his working, is a great source of wealth, for the Holy Spirit is the Spirit of unity, which does not mean uniformity, but that leads everything back to *harmony.* In the Church, it is the Holy Spirit who creates harmony. One

of the Fathers of the Church has an expression I love: the Holy Spirit himself is harmony—*Ipse harmonia est*. He is indeed harmony. Only the Spirit can awaken diversity, plurality, and multiplicity while at the same time building unity. Here too, when we are the ones who try to create diversity and close ourselves up in what makes us different and other, we bring division. When we are the ones who want to build unity in accordance with our human plans, we end up creating uniformity, standardization. But if instead we let ourselves be guided by the Spirit, richness, variety, and diversity never become a source of conflict, because he impels us to experience variety within the communion of the Church. Our journeying together in the Church, under the guidance of her pastors who possess a special charism and ministry, is a sign of the working of the Holy Spirit. Having a sense of the Church is something fundamental for every Christian, every community, and every movement. It is the Church that brings Christ to me, and me to Christ; parallel journeys are very dangerous! When we venture beyond (*proagon*) the Church's teaching and community—the apostle John tells us in his second letter—and do not remain in them, we are not one with the God of Jesus Christ (see 2 John 9). So let us ask ourselves: Am I open to the harmony of the Holy Spirit, overcoming every form of exclusivity? Do I let myself be guided by him, living in the Church and with the Church?

3. A final point. The older theologians used to say that the soul is a kind of sailboat, the Holy Spirit is the wind that fills its sails and drives it forward, and the gusts of wind are the gifts of the Spirit. Lacking his impulse and his grace, we do not go forward. The Holy Spirit draws us into the mystery of the living God and saves us from the threat of a Church that is Gnostic and self-referential, closed in on herself. He impels us to open the doors and go forth to proclaim and bear witness to the good news of the Gospel, to communicate the joy of faith, the encounter with Christ. The Holy Spirit is the soul of *mission*. The events that took place in Jerusalem almost two thousand years ago are not something far removed from us; they are events that affect us and become a lived experience in each of us. The Pentecost of the Upper Room in Jerusalem is the beginning, a beginning that endures. The Holy Spirit is the supreme gift of the risen Christ to his apostles, yet he wants that

gift to reach everyone. In John's Gospel, Jesus says, "I will ask the Father, and he will give you another Advocate to remain with you forever" (John 14:16). It is the Paraclete Spirit, the "Comforter," who grants us the courage to take to the streets of the world, bringing the Gospel! The Holy Spirit makes us look to the horizon and drives us to the very outskirts of existence in order to proclaim life in Jesus Christ. Let us ask ourselves: do we tend to stay closed in on ourselves, on our group, or do we let the Holy Spirit open us to mission? Today let us remember these three words: *newness, harmony,* and *mission.*

PART FOUR

Proclamation and Testimony

13

Do Not Be Afraid

Regina Coeli, 14 April 2013

I would like to reflect briefly on the passage from the Acts of the Apostles (5:12–42) that is read in the Liturgy of this Third Sunday of Easter. This text says that the apostles' first preaching in Jerusalem filled the city with the news that Jesus was truly risen in accordance with the Scriptures and was the Messiah foretold by the prophets. The chief priests and elders of the city were endeavoring to crush the nascent community of believers in Christ and had the apostles thrown into jail, ordering them to stop teaching in his name. But Peter and the other eleven answered, "We must obey God rather than men. The God of our fathers raised Jesus . . . exalted him at his right hand as Leader and Savior. . . . And we are witnesses to these things, and so is the Holy Spirit whom God has given to those who obey him" (Acts 5:29–32). They therefore had the apostles scourged, and once again ordered them to stop speaking in the name of Jesus. And they went away, as Scripture says, "rejoicing that they were counted worthy to suffer dishonor for the name" of Jesus (Acts 5:41).

I ask myself, where did the first disciples find the strength to bear this witness? And that is not all, what was the source of their joy and of their courage to preach despite the obstacles and violence? Let us not forget that the apostles were simple people; they were neither scribes nor doctors of the law, nor did they belong to the class of priests. With their limitations and with the authorities against them, how did they manage to fill Jerusalem with their teaching (see Acts 5:28)? It is clear that only the presence with them of the risen Lord and the action of the Holy Spirit can explain this fact. The Lord who was with them and the Spirit who was impelling them to preach explain this extraordinary fact. Their faith was based on such a strong personal experience of the dead and risen Christ that they feared nothing and no one, and even saw persecution as a cause of honor that enabled them to follow in Jesus' footsteps and to be like him, witnessing with their life.

14

Bringing the Word of God

Homily for the Mass in the Basilica of St. Paul Outside the Walls,
14 April 2013

The strength of Peter and the other apostles strikes us all. In response to the order to be silent, no longer to teach in the name of Jesus, no longer to proclaim his message, they respond clearly: "We must obey God rather than human beings." And they remain undeterred even when flogged, ill-treated, and imprisoned. Peter and the apostles proclaim courageously, fearlessly, what they have received: the Gospel of Jesus. And what about us? Are we capable of bringing the word of God into the environment in which we live? Do we know how to speak of Christ, of what he represents for us, in our families, among the people who form part of our daily lives? Faith is born from listening and is strengthened by proclamation.

But let us take a further step. The proclamation made by Peter and the apostles does not merely consist of words: fidelity to Christ affects their whole lives, which are changed, given a new direction. And it is through their lives that they bear witness to the faith and to the proclamation of Christ. In John's Gospel, Jesus asks Peter three times to feed his flock, to feed it with his love, and he prophesies to him: "When you are old, you will stretch out your hands, and another will gird you and carry you where you do not wish to go" (John 21:18). These words are addressed first and foremost to those of us who are pastors: we cannot feed God's flock unless we let ourselves be carried by God's will even where we would rather not go, unless we are prepared to bear witness to Christ with the gift of ourselves, unreservedly, not in a calculating way, sometimes even at the cost of our lives. But this also applies to everyone: we all have to proclaim and bear witness to the Gospel. We should all ask ourselves: How do I bear witness to Christ through my faith? Do I have the courage of Peter and the other apostles, to think, to choose, and to live as a Christian, obedient to God?

To be sure, the testimony of faith comes in very many forms, just as in a great fresco there is a variety of colors and shades; yet they are all important, even those that do not stand out. In God's great plan, every detail is important, even yours, even my humble little witness, even the hidden witness of those who live their faith with simplicity in everyday family relationships, work relationships, and friendships. There are the saints of every day, the "hidden" saints, a sort of "middle class of holiness," as a French author said, that middle class of holiness to which we can all belong. But in different parts of the world, there are also those who suffer, like Peter and the apostles, on account of the Gospel; there are those who give their lives in order to remain faithful to Christ by means of a witness marked by the shedding of their blood. Let us all remember this: one cannot proclaim the Gospel of Jesus without the tangible witness of one's life. Those who listen to us and observe us must be able to see in our actions what they hear from our lips, and so give glory to God! I am thinking now of some advice that St. Francis of Assisi gave his brothers: preach the Gospel, and if necessary, use words. Preaching with your life, with your witness. Inconsistency on the part of pastors and the faithful between what they say and what they do, between word and manner of life, is undermining the Church's credibility.

But all this is possible only if we recognize Jesus Christ, because it is he who has called us, he who has invited us to travel his path, he who has chosen us. Proclamation and witness are possible only if we are close to him, just as Peter,

> *Proclamation and witness are possible only if we are close to Jesus.*

John, and the other disciples in the passage from John's Gospel were gathered around the risen Jesus; there is a daily closeness to him—they know very well who he is; they know him. The evangelist stresses the fact that "no one dared ask him: 'Who are you?'—they knew it was the Lord" (John 21:12). And this is important for us: living an intense relationship with Jesus, an intimacy of dialogue and of life, in such a way as to recognize him as "the Lord." Worshipping him! The passage that we heard from the book of Revelation speaks to us of worship: the myriads of angels, all creatures, the living beings, the elders, prostrate themselves before the throne of God and of the Lamb that was slain, namely Christ, to whom be praise, honor, and glory (see Rev. 5:11–14). I would like all of us to ask ourselves this question: You, me, do we worship the Lord? Do we turn to God only to ask him for things, to thank him, or do we also turn to him to worship him?

What does it mean, then, to worship God? It means learning to be with him; it means that we stop trying to dialogue with him; and it means sensing that his presence is the truest, the most good, the most important thing of all. All of us, in our own lives, consciously and perhaps sometimes unconsciously, have a very clear order of priority concerning the things we consider important. Worshipping the Lord means giving him the place that he must have; worshipping the Lord means stating, believing—not only by our words—that he alone truly guides our lives. Worshipping the Lord means that we are convinced before him that he is the only God, the God of our lives, the God of our history.

This has a consequence in our lives: we have to empty ourselves of the many small or great idols that we have and in which we take refuge, on which we often seek to base our security. They are idols that we sometimes keep well hidden; they can be ambition, careerism, a taste for success, placing ourselves at the center, the tendency to dominate others, the claim to be the sole masters of our lives, some sins to which we are bound, and many others. I would like a question to resound in the heart of each one of you, and I would like you to answer it honestly: Have I considered which idol lies hidden in my life that prevents me from worshipping the Lord? Worshipping is stripping ourselves of our idols, even the most hidden ones, and choosing the Lord as the center, as the highway of our lives.

15

Called to Proclaim the Gospel

Homily for the Mass with the Brazilian Bishops, 27 July 2013

I wish to reflect with you on three aspects of our vocation: we are called by God, called to proclaim the Gospel, and called to promote the culture of encounter.

1. *Called by God.* I believe that it is important to rekindle constantly an awareness of our divine vocation, which we often take for granted in the midst of our many daily responsibilities: as Jesus says, "You did not choose me, but I chose you" (John 15:16). This means returning to the source of our calling. For this reason, a bishop, a priest, a consecrated person, a seminarian, cannot be "forgetful"; it would mean losing the vital link to that first moment of our journey. Ask for the grace, ask the Virgin for the grace, she who had a good memory; ask for the grace to preserve the memory of this first call. We were called by God, and we were called to be with Jesus (see Mark 3:14), united with him. In reality, this living, this abiding in Christ marks all that we are and all that we do. It is precisely this "life in Christ" that ensures our apostolate is effective, that our service is fruitful: "I appointed you that you should go and bear fruit and that your fruit be authentic" (see John 15:16). It is not creativity, however pastoral it may be, or meetings or planning that ensures our fruitfulness, even if these are greatly helpful. But what ensures our fruitfulness is our being faithful to Jesus, who says insistently: "Abide in me and I in you" (John 15:4). And we know well what that means: to contemplate him, to worship him, to

embrace him, in our daily encounter with him in the Eucharist, in our life of prayer, in our moments of adoration; it means to recognize him present and to embrace him in those most in need. "Being with" Christ does not mean isolating ourselves from others. Rather, it is a "being with" in order to go forth and encounter others. Here I wish to recall some words of Blessed Teresa of Calcutta. She said: "We must be very proud of our vocation because it gives us the opportunity to serve Christ in the poor. It is in the *favelas* . . . in the *villas miseria* that one must go to seek and to serve Christ. We must go to them as the priest presents himself at the altar, with joy" (*Mother's Instructions*, Blessed Teresa of Calcutta, 1:80). Jesus is the Good Shepherd; he is our true treasure. Please, let us not erase Jesus from our lives! Let us ground our hearts ever more in him (see Luke 12:34).

2. *Called to proclaim the Gospel.* Many of you, dear bishops and priests, if not all, have accompanied your young people to World Youth Day. They too have heard the mandate of Jesus: "Go and make disciples of all nations" (see Matt. 28:19). It is our responsibility as pastors to help kindle within their hearts the desire to be missionary disciples of Jesus. Certainly this invitation could cause many to feel somewhat afraid, thinking that to be missionaries requires leaving their own homes and countries, family and friends. God asks us to be missionaries. But where—where he himself places us, in our own countries or wherever he has chosen for us. Let us help the young. Let us have an attentive ear to listen to their dreams—they need to be heard—to listen to their successes, to pay attention to their difficulties. You have to sit down and listen to the same libretto, but accompanied by diverse music, with different characteristics. Having the patience to listen! I ask this of you with all my heart! In the confessional, in spiritual direction, in accompanying. Let us find ways to spend time with them. Planting seeds is demanding and very tiring, very tiring! It is much more rewarding to enjoy the harvest! How cunning! Reaping is more enjoyable for us! But Jesus asks us to sow with care and responsibility.

Let us spare no effort in the formation of our young people! St. Paul used an expression that he embodied in his own life, when he addressed the Christian community: "My little children, with whom I am again in travail until Christ be formed in you" (Gal. 4:19). Let us embody this also in our own ministry! Helping our young people discover the courage and joy of faith, the

We cannot keep ourselves shut up in parishes, in our communities, in our parish or diocesan institutions, when so many people are waiting for the Gospel!

joy of being loved personally by God, is very difficult. But when young people understand it, when young people experience it through the anointing of the Holy Spirit, this "being personally loved by God" accompanies them for the rest of their lives. They rediscover the joy that God gave his Son Jesus for our salvation. Let us form them in mission, to go out, to go forth, to be itinerants who communicate the faith. Jesus did this with his own disciples; he did not keep them under his wing like a hen with her chicks. He sent them out! We cannot keep ourselves shut up in parishes, in our communities, in our parish or diocesan institutions, when so many people are waiting for the Gospel! To go out as ones sent. It is not enough simply to open the door in welcome because they come, but we must go out through that door to seek and meet the people! Let us urge our young people to go forth. Of course, they will make mistakes, but let us not be afraid! The apostles made mistakes before us. Let us urge them to go forth. Let us think resolutely about pastoral needs, beginning on the outskirts, with those who are farthest away, with those who do not usually go to church. They are the VIPs who are invited. Go and search for them at the crossroads.

3. To be called by Jesus, to be called to evangelize, and third: to be *called to promote the culture of encounter.* In many places, generally speaking, because of the economic humanism that has been imposed in the world, the culture of exclusion, of rejection, is spreading. There is no place for the elderly or for the unwanted child; there is no time for that poor person in the street. At times, it seems that for some people, human relations are regulated by two modern "dogmas": efficiency and pragmatism. Dear bishops, priests, religious, and you seminarians who are preparing for ministry—have

the courage to go against the tide of this culture. Be courageous! Remember this, which helps me a great deal and on which I meditate frequently: take the first book of Maccabees, and recall how many of the people wanted to adapt to the culture of the time: *No . . .! Leave us alone! Let us eat of everything, like the others do . . . Fine, yes to the Law, but not every part of it . . .* And they ended up abandoning the faith and placing themselves in the current of that culture. Have the courage to go against the tide of this culture of efficiency, this culture of waste. Encountering and welcoming everyone, [building] solidarity—a word that is being hidden by this culture, as if it were a bad word—solidarity and fraternity: these are what make our society truly human.

Be servants of communion and of the culture of encounter! I would like you to be almost obsessed about this. Be so without being presumptuous, imposing "our truths," but rather be guided by the humble yet joyful certainty of those who have been found, touched, and transformed by the Truth who is Christ, ever to be proclaimed (see Luke 24:13–35).

16

Conveying Hope and Joy

Homily at the Basilica of the Shrine of Our Lady of the Conception of Aparecida, 24 July 2013

I would like to speak of three simple attitudes: hopefulness, openness to being surprised by God, and living in joy.

Hopefulness. The second reading of the Mass presents a dramatic scene: a woman—an image of Mary and the Church—is being pursued by a dragon, the devil, who wants to devour her child. But the scene is not one of death but of life, because God intervenes and saves the child (see Rev. 12:13a, 15–16a). How many difficulties are present in the life of every individual, among our people, in our communities; yet as great as these may seem, God never allows us to be overwhelmed by them. In the face of those moments of discouragement we experience in life, in our efforts to evangelize or to embody our faith as parents within the family, I would like to say forcefully: always know in your heart that God is by your side; he never abandons you! Let us never lose hope! Let us never allow it to die in our hearts! The "dragon," evil, is present in our history, but it does not have the upper hand. The one with the upper hand is God, and God is our hope! It is true that nowadays, to some extent, everyone, including our young people, feels attracted by the many idols that take the place of God and appear to offer hope: money, success, power, pleasure. Often a growing sense of loneliness and emptiness in the hearts of many people leads them to

> **Let us never lose hope! Let us never allow it to die in our hearts!**

seek satisfaction in these ephemeral idols. Dear brothers and sisters, let us be lights of hope! Let us maintain a positive outlook on reality. Let us encourage the generosity that is typical of the young and help them to work actively in building a better world. Young people are a powerful engine for the Church and for society. They do not need material things alone; also and above all, they need to have held up to them those nonmaterial values that are the spiritual heart of a people, the memory of a people. In this shrine, which is part of the memory of Brazil, we can almost read those values: spirituality, generosity, solidarity, perseverance, fraternity, joy; they are values whose deepest root is in the Christian faith.

The second attitude: *openness to being surprised by God.* Anyone who is a man or a woman of hope—the great hope that faith gives us—knows that even in the midst of difficulties God acts and surprises us. The history of this shrine is a good example: three fishermen, after a day of catching no fish, found something unexpected in the waters of the Parnaíba River: an image of Our Lady of the Immaculate Conception. Whoever would have thought that the site of a fruitless fishing expedition would become the place where all Brazilians can feel that they are children of one Mother? God always surprises us, like the new wine in the Gospel. God always saves the best for us. But he asks us to let ourselves be surprised by his love, to accept his surprises. Let us trust God! [When we are] cut off from him, the wine of joy, the wine of hope, runs out. If we draw near to him, if we stay with him, what seems to be cold water, difficulty, sin, is changed into the new wine of friendship with him.

The third attitude: *living in joy.* Dear friends, if we walk in hope, allowing ourselves to be surprised by the new wine that Jesus offers us, we have joy in our hearts, and we cannot fail to be witnesses of this joy. Christians are joyful; they are never gloomy. God is at our side. We have a Mother who always intercedes for the life of her children, for us, as Queen Esther did in the first reading (see Esther 5:3). Jesus has shown us that the face of God is that of a loving Father. Sin and death have been defeated. Christians cannot be pessimists! They do not look like someone in constant mourning. If we are truly

17

Giving All

Homily at the Profession of Faith with the Bishops of the Italian Episcopal Conference, 23 May 2013

The One who scrutinizes hearts (see Rom. 8:27) makes himself a beggar of love and questions us on the one truly essential issue, a premise and condition for feeding his sheep, his lambs, his Church. May every ministry be based on this intimacy with the Lord; living from him is the measure of our ecclesial service, which is expressed in the readiness to obey, to humble ourselves, as we heard in the letter to the Philippians, and for the total gift of self (see Phil. 2:6–11).

Moreover, the consequence of loving the Lord is giving everything—truly everything, even our life—for him. This is what must distinguish our pastoral ministry; it is the litmus test that tells us how deeply we have embraced the gift received in responding to Jesus' call, and how closely bound we are to the individuals and communities that have been entrusted to our care. We are not the expression of a structure or of an organizational need: even with the service of our authority we are called to be a sign of the presence and action of the risen Lord, and thus to build up the community in love.

Not that this should be taken for granted: even the greatest love, in fact, when it is not constantly nourished, weakens and fades away. Not for nothing did the apostle Paul recommend: "take heed to yourselves and to all the flock, in which the Holy Spirit has made you guardians, to feed the church of the Lord which he obtained with his own Son's blood" (see Acts 20:28).

A lack of vigilance—as we know—makes the pastor tepid; it makes him absent-minded, forgetful, and even impatient. It tantalizes him with the prospect of a career, the enticement of money, and with compromises with a mundane spirit; it makes him lazy, turning him into an official, a state functionary concerned with himself, with organization and structures, rather than with the true good of the People of God. Then one runs the risk of denying the Lord, as did the apostle Peter, even if he formally presents him and speaks in his name; one obscures the holiness of the hierarchical Mother Church, making her less fruitful.

Who are we before God? What are our trials? We have so many; we each have our own. What is God saying to us through them? What are we relying on in order to surmount them?

Just as it was for Peter, Jesus' insistent and heartfelt question can leave us pained and more aware of the weakness of our freedom, threatened as it is by thousands of interior and exterior forms of conditioning that all too often give rise to bewilderment, frustration, and even disbelief.

These are not of course the sentiments and attitudes that the Lord wants to inspire; rather, the enemy, the devil, takes advantage of them to isolate us in bitterness, complaint, and despair.

Jesus, the Good Shepherd, does not humiliate or abandon people to remorse. Through him the tenderness of the Father, who consoles and revitalizes, speaks; it is he who brings us from the disintegration of shame—because shame truly breaks us up—to the fabric of trust. He restores courage, re-entrusts responsibility, and sends us out on mission.

Peter, purified in the crucible of forgiveness, could say humbly, "Lord, you know everything; you know that I love you" (John 21:17). I am sure that we can all say this with heartfelt feeling. And Peter, purified, urges us in his first letter to tend "the flock of God . . . not by constraint but willingly, not for shameful gain but eagerly, not as domineering over those in your charge but being examples to the flock" (1 Pet. 5:2–3).

Yes, being pastors means believing every day in the grace and strength that come to us from the Lord despite our weakness, and wholly assuming the responsibility for walking before the flock, relieved of the burdens that obstruct healthy apostolic promptness, hesitant leadership, so as to make our voice recognizable both to those who have embraced the faith and to those who "are not [yet] of this fold" (John 10:16). We are called to make our own the dream of God, whose house knows no exclusion of people or peoples, as Isaiah prophetically foretold (see Isa. 2:2–5).

For this reason, being pastors also means being prepared to walk among and behind the flock; being capable of listening to the silent tale of those who are suffering and of sustaining the steps of those who fear they may not make it; attentive to raising, to reassuring, and to instilling hope. Our faith emerges strengthened from

> *Let us therefore set aside every form of arrogance, to bend down to all whom the Lord has entrusted to our care.*

sharing with the lowly. Let us therefore set aside every form of arrogance, to bend down to all whom the Lord has entrusted to our care.

PART FIVE

Full-Time Christians

18

Coming Out of Ourselves

General Audience, 27 March 2013

What does being a Christian mean? What does following Jesus on his journey to Calvary on his way to the cross and the resurrection mean? In his earthly mission Jesus walked the roads of the Holy Land; he called twelve simple people to stay with him, to share his journey, and to continue his mission. He chose them from among the people full of faith in God's promises. He spoke to all without distinction: the great and the lowly, the rich young man and the poor widow, the powerful and the weak; he brought God's mercy and forgiveness; he healed, he comforted, he understood; he gave hope; he brought to all the presence of God who cares for every man and every woman, just as a good father and a good mother care for each one of their children. God does not wait for us to go to him, but it is he who moves toward us, without calculation, without quantification. That is what God is like. He always takes the first step; he comes toward us. Jesus lived the daily reality of the most ordinary people: he was moved as he faced the crowd that seemed like a flock without a shepherd; he wept before the sorrow that Martha and Mary felt at the death of their brother, Lazarus; he called a publican to be his disciple; he also suffered betrayal by a friend. In him God has given us the certitude that he is with us, that he is among us. "Foxes," Jesus said, "have holes, and birds of the air have nests, but the Son of man has nowhere to lay his head" (Matt. 8:20). Jesus has no house, because his house is the people; it is we who are his dwelling place; his mission is to open God's doors to all, to be the

71

presence of God's love. In Holy Week we live the crowning moment of this journey, of this plan of love that runs through the entire history of the relations between God and humanity. Jesus enters Jerusalem to take his last step, with which he sums up the whole of his existence. He gives himself without reserve; he keeps nothing for himself, not even life. At the Last Supper, with his friends, he breaks the bread and passes the cup around "for us." The Son of God offers himself to us; he puts his body and his blood into our hands, so as to be with us always, to dwell among us. And in the Garden of Olives, and likewise in the trial before Pilate, he puts up no resistance, he gives himself; he is the suffering Servant, foretold by Isaiah, who empties himself, even unto death (see Isa. 53:12).

Jesus does not experience this love that leads to his sacrifice passively or as a fatal destiny. He does not, of course, conceal his deep human distress as he faces a violent death, but with absolute trust he commends himself to the Father. Jesus gave himself up to death voluntarily in order to reciprocate the love of God the Father, in perfect union with his will, to demonstrate his love for us. On the cross Jesus "loved me and gave himself for me" (Gal. 2:20). Each one of us can say, "He loved me and gave himself for me." Each one can say this "for me."

What is the meaning of all this for us? It means that this is my, your, and our road too—living Holy Week, following Jesus not only with the emotion of the heart. Living Holy Week, following Jesus, means learning to come out of ourselves in order to go to meet others, to go toward the outskirts of existence, to be the first to take a step toward our brothers and sisters, especially those who are the most distant, those who are forgotten, those who are most in need of understanding, comfort, and help. There is such a great need to bring the living presence of Jesus, merciful and full of love!

Living Holy Week means entering ever more deeply into the logic of God, into the logic of the cross, which is not primarily that of suffering and death, but rather that of love and of the gift of self that brings life. It means entering into the logic of the Gospel. Following and accompanying Christ, staying with him, demands "coming out of ourselves," requires us to be outgoing; to come out of a dreary way of living faith that has become a habit, out of the temptation to withdraw into our own plans, which end by shutting out God's creative action. God came out of himself to come among us; he pitched his tent among us to bring to us his mercy that saves and gives hope. Nor must we be satisfied with staying in the pen of the ninety-nine sheep if we want to follow him and to remain with him; we too must "go out" with him to seek the lost sheep, the one that has strayed the furthest. Be sure to remember: [we need to come] out of ourselves, just as God came out of himself in Jesus and Jesus came out of himself for all of us.

Someone might say to me, "But Father, I don't have time," "I have so many things to do," "It's difficult," "What can I do with my feeble-

God always thinks mercifully.

ness and my sins, with so many things?" We are often satisfied with a few prayers, with a distracted and sporadic participation in Sunday Mass, with a few charitable acts; but we do not have the courage "to come out" to bring Christ to others. We are a bit like St. Peter. As soon as Jesus speaks of his Passion, death, and resurrection, of the gift of himself, of love for all, the apostle takes him aside and reproaches him. What Jesus says upsets his plans, seems unacceptable, threatens the security he had built for himself, his idea of the Messiah. And Jesus looks at his disciples and addresses to Peter what may possibly be the harshest words in the Gospels: "Get behind me Satan! For you are not on the side of God, but of human beings" (Mark 8:33). God always thinks with mercy: do not forget this. God always thinks mercifully. He is the merciful Father! God thinks like the father waiting for the son and who goes to meet him when he spots him coming when he is still far off . . . What does this mean? That he went every day to see if his son was coming home: this is our merciful Father. It indicates that he was waiting for him with longing on the terrace of his house. God thinks like the Samaritan who did not pass by the unfortunate man, pitying him or looking at him from the other side of the road, but helped him without asking for anything in return—without asking whether he was a Jew, a pagan, or a Samaritan, whether he was rich or poor: he asked for nothing. He went to help him; God is like this. God thinks like the shepherd who lays down his life in order to defend and save his sheep.

19

Walking

Address to the Clergy in the Cathedral of San Rufino in Assisi, Italy, 4 October 2013

[*Walking*] is one of my favorite words when I think about a Christian and about the Church. However, it has a special meaning for you: you are about to enter into the diocesan synod. To hold a "synod" means to walk together. I think this is truly the most wonderful experience we can have: to belong to a people walking, journeying through history together with our Lord, who walks among us! We are not alone; we do not walk alone. We are part of the one flock of Christ that walks together.

Here I think once more of you priests, and let me place myself in your company. What could be more beautiful for us than walking with our people? It is beautiful! When I think of the parish priests who knew the names of their parishioners, who went to visit them: one of them told me, "I know the name of each family's dog." They even knew the dog's name! How nice it was! What could be more beautiful than this? I repeat it often: walking with our people, sometimes in front, sometimes behind, and sometimes in the middle. We walk in front in order to guide the community, in the middle in order to encourage and support, and at the back so that no one lags too far behind, to keep them united. There is another reason too: because the people have a "nose"! The people scent out, discover, new ways to walk; they have the *sensus fidei*, as theologians call it. What could be more beautiful than this?

During the synod, it will be very important to consider what the Holy Spirit is saying to the laity, to the People of God, to everyone.

But the most important thing is to walk together by working together, by helping one another, by asking forgiveness, by acknowledging one's mistakes and asking for forgiveness, and also by accepting the apologies of others by forgiving—how important this is! Sometimes I think of married people who separate after many years. "Oh . . . no, we didn't understand each other. We drifted apart." Perhaps at times they didn't know how to ask for forgiveness at the right time. Perhaps at times they did not know how to forgive. And I always give this advice to newlyweds: "Argue as much as you like. If the plates fly, let them! But never end the day without making peace! Never!" And if married people learn to say, "Excuse me, I was tired," or even a little gesture, this is peace. Then carry on with life the next day. This is a beautiful secret, and it prevents these painful separations. It is important to walk in unity, without running ahead, without nostalgia for the past. And while you walk you talk, you get to know one another, you tell one other about yourselves, you grow as a family. Here let us ask ourselves: How do we walk? How does our diocese walk? Does it walk together? And what am I doing so that it may truly walk in unity?

20

Taking the Cross

Homily on Palm Sunday, 24 March 2013

Jesus enters Jerusalem. The crowd of disciples accompanies him in festive mood, their garments stretched out before him. There is talk of the miracles he has accomplished, and loud praises are heard: "Blessed is the King who comes in the name of the Lord. Peace in heaven and glory in the highest!" (Luke 19:38).

Crowds, celebration, praise, blessing, peace: joy fills the air. Jesus has awakened great hopes, especially in the hearts of the simple, the humble, the poor, the forgotten, those who do not matter in the eyes of the world. He understands human sufferings, he has shown the face of God's mercy, and he has bent down to heal body and soul.

This is Jesus. This is his heart, which looks to all of us, to our sicknesses, to our sins. The love of Jesus is great. And thus he enters Jerusalem, with this love, and looks at us. It is a beautiful scene, full of light—the light of the love of Jesus, the love of his heart—of joy, of celebration.

At the beginning of Mass, we too repeated it. We waved our palms, our olive branches. We too welcomed Jesus; we too expressed our joy at accompanying him, at knowing him to be close, present in us and among us as a friend, a brother, and also as a King—that is, a shining beacon for our lives. Jesus is God, but he lowered himself to walk with us. He is our

This joy is born from knowing that with him we are never alone, even at difficult moments.

friend, our brother. He illumines our path here. And in this way we have welcomed him today. And here the first word that I wish to say to you: *joy*! Do not be men and women of sadness: a Christian can never be sad! Never give way to discouragement! Ours is not a joy born of having many possessions, but of having encountered a Person: Jesus, in our midst. This joy is born from knowing that with him we are never alone, even at difficult moments, even when our life's journey comes up against problems and obstacles that seem insurmountable—and there are so many of them! And in this moment the enemy, the devil, comes, often disguised as an angel, and slyly speaks his word to us. Do not listen to him! Let us follow Jesus! We accompany, we follow Jesus, but above all we know that he accompanies us and carries us on his shoulders. This is our joy; this is the hope that we must bring to this world. Please do not let yourselves be robbed of hope! Do not let hope be stolen! The hope that Jesus gives us.

Why does Jesus enter Jerusalem? Or better: how does Jesus enter Jerusalem? The crowds acclaim him as King. And he does not deny it; he does not tell them to be silent (see Luke 19:39–40). But what kind of a King is Jesus? Let us take a look at him: he is riding on a donkey, he is not accompanied by a court, he is not surrounded by an army as a symbol of power. He is received by humble people, simple folk who have the sense to see something more in Jesus; they have that sense of the faith which says, "Here is the Savior." Jesus does not enter the Holy City to receive the honors reserved for earthly kings, to the powerful, to rulers; he enters to be scourged, insulted, and abused, as Isaiah foretold (see Isa. 50:6). He enters to receive a crown of thorns, a staff, a purple robe: his kingship becomes an object of derision. He enters to climb Calvary, carrying his burden of wood.

And this brings us to the second word: *cross*. Jesus enters Jerusalem in order to die on the cross. And it is precisely here that his kingship shines forth in godly fashion: his royal throne is the wood of the cross! It reminds me of what Benedict XVI said to the cardinals: you are princes, but of a King crucified. That is the throne of Jesus. Jesus takes it upon himself . . . Why the cross? Because Jesus takes upon himself the evil, the filth, the sin of the world, including the sin of all of us, and he cleanses it; he cleanses it with his blood, with the mercy and the love of God. Let us look around: how many wounds are inflicted upon humanity by evil! Wars, violence, economic conflicts that hit the weakest, greed for money that you can't take with you and have to leave. When we were small, our grandmother used to say, "A shroud has no pocket." Love of power, corruption, divisions, crimes against human life and against creation! And—as each one of us knows and is aware—our personal sins: our failures in love and respect toward God, our neighbor and the whole of creation. Jesus on the cross feels the whole weight of the evil, and with the force of God's love he conquers it; he defeats it with his resurrection. This is the good that Jesus does for us on the throne of the cross. Christ's cross, embraced with love, never leads to sadness, but to joy, to the joy of having been saved and of doing a little of what he did on the day of his death.

21

Evangelizing

General Audience, 22 May 2013

Evangelizing is the Church's mission. It is not the mission of only a few, but it is mine, yours, and our mission. The apostle Paul exclaimed, "Woe to me if I do not preach the Gospel!" (1 Cor. 9:16). We must all be evangelizers, especially with our lives! Paul VI stressed that "evangelizing is . . . the grace and vocation proper to the Church, her deepest identity. She exists in order to evangelize" (apostolic exhortation, *Evangelii nuntiandi*, no. 14).

Who is the real driving force of evangelization in our life and in the Church? Paul VI wrote clearly: "It is the Holy Spirit who today, just as at the beginning of the Church, acts in every evangelizer who allows himself to be possessed and led by him. The Holy Spirit places on his lips the words which he could not find by himself, and at the same time the Holy Spirit predisposes the soul of the hearer to be open and receptive to the Good News and to the Kingdom being proclaimed" (*Evangelii nuntiandi*, no. 75). To evangelize, therefore, it is necessary to open ourselves once again to the horizon of God's Spirit, without being afraid of what he asks us or of where he leads us. Let us entrust ourselves to him! He will enable us to live out and bear witness to our faith, and will illuminate the hearts of those we meet. This was the experience at Pentecost. "There appeared" to the apostles gathered in the Upper Room with Mary "tongues as of fire, distributed and resting on each one of them. And they were all filled with the Holy Spirit and began to speak in other tongues, as the Spirit gave them utterance" (Acts 2:3–4). In coming down upon the apostles, the Holy Spirit makes them leave the room they had locked themselves into out of fear; he prompts them to step out of themselves and transforms them into heralds and witnesses of the "mighty works of God" (Acts 2:11). Moreover, this transformation brought about by the Holy Spirit reverberated in the multitude that had arrived "from every nation under heaven" (Acts 2:5), for each one heard the apostles' words as if they had been "speaking in his own language" (Acts 2:6).

This is one of the first important effects of the action of the Holy Spirit, who guides and brings to life the proclamation of the Gospel: unity, communion. It was in Babel, according to the biblical account, that the dispersion of people and the confusion of languages had begun, the results of the act of pride and conceit of people who wanted to build with their efforts alone, without God, "a city, and a tower with its top in the heavens" (Gen. 11:4). At Pentecost these divisions were overcome. There was no longer conceit with regard to God, nor the closure of some people to others; instead, there was openness to God, there was going out to proclaim his word: a new language, that of love, which the Holy Spirit pours out into our hearts (see Rom. 5:5), a language that all can understand and that, once received, can be expressed in every life and every culture. The language of the Spirit, the language of the Gospel, is the language of communion that invites us to get the better of closedness and indifference, division and antagonism.

We must all ask ourselves: How do I let myself be guided by the Holy Spirit in such a way that my life and my witness of faith are both unity and communion? Do I convey the word of reconciliation and of love, which is the Gospel, to the milieus in which I live? At times it seems that we are repeating today what happened at Babel: division, the incapacity to understand one another, rivalry, envy, egoism. What do I do with my life? Do I create unity around me? Or do I cause division by gossip, criticism, or envy? What do I do? Let us think about this. Spreading the Gospel means that we are the first to proclaim and live the reconciliation, forgiveness, peace, unity, and love that the Holy Spirit gives us.

> *What do I do with my life? Do I create unity around me? Or do I cause division by gossip, criticism, or envy?*

Let us remember Jesus' words: "it is by your love for one another, that everyone will recognize you as my disciples, if you have love for one another" (John 13: 34–35).

A second element is the day of Pentecost. Peter, filled with the Holy Spirit and standing "with the eleven," "lifted up his voice" (Acts 2:14) and "confidently" (Acts 2:29) proclaimed the Good News of Jesus, who gave his life for our salvation and whom God raised from the dead. This is another effect of the Holy Spirit's action: the courage to proclaim the newness of the Gospel of Jesus to all, confidently (with parrhesia) in a loud voice, in every time and in every place. Today too this happens for the Church and for each one of us: the fire of Pentecost, from the action of the Holy Spirit, releases an ever-new energy for mission, new ways in which to proclaim the message of salvation, new courage for evangelizing. Let us never close ourselves to this action! Let us live the Gospel humbly and courageously! Let us witness to the newness, hope, and joy that the Lord brings to life. Let us feel within us "the delightful and comforting joy of evangelizing" (Paul VI, *Evangelii nuntiandi*, no. 80). Because evangelizing, proclaiming Jesus, gives us joy. In contrast, egoism makes us bitter, sad, and depresses us. Evangelizing uplifts us.

I will only mention a third element, which, however, is particularly important: a new evangelization, a Church that evangelizes, must always start with prayer, with asking, as the apostles did in the Upper Room, for the fire of the Holy Spirit. Only a faithful and intense relationship with God makes it possible to get out of our own closedness and proclaim the Gospel with parrhesia. Without prayer our acts are empty and our proclamation has no soul; it is not inspired by the Spirit.

PART SIX

Shepherds with the "Odor of the Sheep"

22

To Be a Pastor

Address to a Group of Newly Appointed Bishops Taking Part in a Conference, 19 September 2013

"Tend the flock of God that is your charge, not by constraint but willingly, not for shameful gain but eagerly, not as domineering over those in your charge but being examples to the flock" (1 Pet. 5:2). May St. Peter's words be engraved on our heart! We are called and constituted pastors, not pastors by ourselves but by the Lord; and not to serve ourselves but the flock that has been entrusted to us, and to serve it to the point of laying down our life, like Christ, the Good Shepherd (see John 10:11).

What does tending and having the "permanent and daily care of their sheep" (Second Vatican Ecumenical Council, *Lumen gentium*, no. 27) actually mean? Three brief thoughts. Tending means welcoming magnanimously, walking with the flock, and staying with the flock. Welcoming, walking, staying.

1. *To welcome magnanimously*. May your heart be large enough to welcome all the men and women you come across during the day and whom you go and seek out when you go about your parishes and to every community. Ask yourselves from this moment: how will those who knock at my door find it? If they find it open, through your kindness, your availability, they will experience God's fatherhood and will understand that the Church is a good mother who always welcomes and loves.

2. *To walk with the flock.* To welcome magnanimously, and to walk. Welcoming everyone in order to walk with everyone. The bishop journeys *with* and *among* his flock. This means setting out with one's faithful and with all those who turn to you, sharing in their joys and hopes, their difficulties and sufferings, as brothers and as friends, but especially as fathers who can listen, understand, help, and guide. Walking together demands love, and ours is a service of love, *amoris officium*, as St. Augustine used to say (*In evangelium Johannis tractatus* 123, 5: *PL* 35, 1967).

a) And as you walk I would like to remember *affection for your priests*. Your priests are your first neighbor; the priest is the bishop's first neighbor—love your neighbor, but he is your first neighbor—your priests are indispensable collaborators from whom to seek counsel and help and for whom you should care as fathers, brothers, and friends. One of your priorities is the spiritual care of the presbyterate, but do not forget the human needs of each individual priest, especially in the most delicate and important events in their ministry and their life. The time you spend with your priests is never wasted! Receive them whenever they ask you to. Do not let a telephone call go unanswered. I have heard priests say [when I was directing them] during the Spiritual Exercises—I don't know whether it's true but I've heard it very often in my life—"Well! I called the bishop, and his secretary told me that he had no time to receive me!" It was like this for months and months and months. I don't know whether it is true, but if a priest telephones the bishop, then that same day or at least the following day, the call [should be returned]: "I heard that you called; what would you like? I cannot receive you today but let's look at the dates together." Please listen to what the father says. Vice versa, the priest might think: "But he doesn't care; he is not a father, he is an office head!" Think about this well. This would be a good resolution: reply to a telephone call from a priest, if [not on the same day], then at least the following day. And then see when you can meet him. Be constantly close; be in touch with them all the time.

b) Then *presence in the diocese*. In the homily in the Chrism Mass this year, I said that pastors must have "the odor of sheep." Be pastors with the odor of the sheep, present in your people's midst like Jesus, the Good Shepherd. Your presence is not secondary; it is indispensable. Pres-

> *A bishop who lives among his faithful has his ears open to listen to "what the Spirit says to the churches."*

ence! The people themselves, who want to see their bishop walk with them and be near them, ask it of you. They need his presence in order to live and breathe! Do not close yourselves in! Go down among your faithful, even into the margins of your dioceses and into all those "peripheries of existence" where there is suffering, loneliness, and human degradation. A pastoral presence means walking with the People of God, walking in front of them, showing them the way, showing them the path; walking in their midst, to strengthen them in unity; walking behind them, to make sure no one gets left behind, but especially, never to lose the scent of the People of God in order to find new roads. A bishop who lives among his faithful has his ears open to listen to "what the Spirit says to the churches" (Rev. 2:7), and to the "voice of the sheep," also through those diocesan institutions whose task it is to advise the bishop, promoting a loyal and constructive dialogue. It is impossible to think of a bishop who did not have these diocesan institutions: a presbyteral council, consultors, a pastoral council, a council for financial matters. This means really being with the people. This pastoral presence will enable you to be thoroughly acquainted with the culture, customs, and mores of the area, the wealth of holiness that is present there. Immerse yourselves in your own flock!

c) And here I would like to add: let your *style of service* to the flock be that of humility; I would say even of austerity and essentiality. Please, we pastors are not men with the "psychology of princes"—please—ambitious men who are bridegrooms of this Church while awaiting another that is more beautiful, wealthier. But this is a scandal! If a penitent arrives and says to you, "I am married. I live with my wife, but I am always looking at that woman who is more beautiful than mine: is this a sin, Father?" The Gospel says: it is a sin of adultery. Is there a "spiritual adultery"? I don't know; think about it. Do not wait for another more beautiful, more important, or richer. Be careful not to slip into the spirit of careerism! That really is a form of cancer! It is not only with words but also and above all with a practical witness in our life that we are teachers and educators of our people. The proclamation of faith requires us to live out what we teach. Mission and life are inseparable (see John Paul II, *Pastores gregis*, no. 31). This is a question we should ask ourselves every day: do I practice what I preach?

3. To welcome, to walk. And the third and last element: *staying with the flock*. I am referring to *stability*, which has two precise aspects: "staying" in the diocese and staying in "this" diocese, as I said, without seeking change or promotion. As pastors it is impossible to know your flock really well—walking in front of it, in its midst and behind it, caring for it with your teaching, with the administration of the sacraments and with the testimony of your life—unless you remain in your diocese. In this, the Council of Trent is very up to date: residence. Ours is a time in which we can travel and move from one place to another easily, a time when communications are rapid, the epoch of the Internet. However, the old law of residence is not out of fashion! It is necessary for good pastoral government (directory, *Apostolorum successores*, no. 161). Of course, concern for other Churches and for the universal Church can take you from your diocese, but let it be only for the time that is strictly necessary and not a regular practice. You see, residence is not only required for the purpose of good organization, it is not a functional element; it has a theological root! You are bridegrooms of your communities, deeply bound to them! I ask you, please remain among your people. Stay, stay . . . Steer clear of the scandal of being "airport bishops"! Be welcoming pastors, journeying on with your people, with affection, with mercy, treating them with gentleness and fatherly firmness, with humility and discretion. And may you also be able to see your own limitations and have a large dose of good humor. This is a grace we bishops must ask for. We must all ask for this grace: Lord, give me a sense of humor. Finding the way to laugh at oneself first is part of it. And stay with your flock!

23

Priests Who Come to Serve

Homily, 21 April 2013

It is true that God has made his entire holy people a royal priesthood in Christ. Nevertheless, our great Priest himself, Jesus Christ, chose certain disciples to carry out publicly in his name, and on behalf of humankind, a priestly office in the Church. For Christ was sent by the Father, and he in turn sent the apostles into the world, so that through them and their successors, the bishops, he might continue to exercise his office of Teacher, Priest, and Shepherd.

Indeed, priests are established coworkers of the Order of Bishops, with whom they are joined in the priestly office and with whom they are called to the service of the people of God.

After mature deliberation and prayer, these, our brothers, are now to be ordained to the priesthood in the order of the presbyterate so as to serve Christ the Teacher, Priest, and Shepherd, by whose ministry his body, that is, the Church, is built and grows into the people of God, a holy temple.

In being configured to Christ, the eternal High Priest, and joined to the priesthood of the bishops, they will be consecrated as true priests of the New Testament, to preach the Gospel, to shepherd God's people, and to celebrate the sacred Liturgy, especially the Lord's sacrifice.

Now, my dear brothers and sons, you are to be raised to the Order of the Priesthood. For your part you will exercise the sacred duty of teaching in the name of Christ the Teacher. Impart to everyone the word of God that you have received with joy. Remember your mothers, your grandmothers, your catechists, who gave you the word of God, the faith . . . the gift of faith! They transmitted to you this gift of faith. Meditating on the law of the Lord, see that you believe what you read, that you teach what you believe, and that you practice what you teach. Remember too that the word of God is not your property: it is the word of God. And the Church is the custodian of the word of God.

In this way, let what you teach be nourishment for the people of God. Let the holiness of your lives be a delightful fragrance to Christ's faithful, so that by word and example you may

> *Let what you teach be nourishment for the people of God.*

build up the house that is God's Church. Likewise you will exercise in Christ the office of sanctifying. For by your ministry the spiritual sacrifice of the faithful will be made perfect, being united to the sacrifice of Christ, which will be offered through your hands in an unbloody way on the altar, in union with the faithful, in the celebration of the sacraments.

Understand, therefore, what you do, and imitate what you celebrate. As celebrants of the mystery of the Lord's death and resurrection, strive to put to death whatever in your members is sinful and to walk in newness of life.

You will gather others into the people of God through baptism, and you will forgive sins in the name of Christ and the Church in the sacrament of penance. Today I ask you in the name of Christ and the Church, never tire of being merciful. You will comfort the sick and the elderly with holy oil: do not hesitate to show tenderness toward the elderly. When you celebrate the sacred rites, when you offer prayers of praise and thanks to God throughout the hours of the day, not only for the people of God but for the world—remember then that you are taken from among men and appointed on their behalf for those things that pertain to God.

Therefore, carry out the ministry of Christ the Priest with constant joy and genuine love, attending not to your own concerns but to those of Jesus Christ. You are pastors, not functionaries. Be mediators, not intermediaries.

Finally, dear sons, exercising for your part the office of Christ, Head and Shepherd, while united with the bishop and subject to him, strive to bring the faithful together into one family, so that you may lead them to God the Father through Christ in the Holy Spirit. Keep always before your eyes the example of the Good Shepherd, who came not to be served but to serve, and who came to seek out and save what was lost.

24

The Anointing of the People

Homily at the Chrism Mass, 28 March 2013

The Bible often speaks of God's "anointed ones": the suffering Servant of Isaiah, King David, and Jesus our Lord. All three have this in common: the anointing that they receive is meant in turn to anoint God's faithful people, whose servants they are; they are anointed for the poor, for prisoners, for the oppressed . . . A fine image of this "being for" others can be found in Psalm 133: "It is like the precious oil upon the head, running down upon the beard, on the beard of Aaron, running down upon the collar of his robe" (Psalm 133:2). The image of spreading oil, flowing down from the beard of Aaron upon the collar of his sacred robe, is an image of the priestly anointing that, through Christ, the Anointed One, reaches the ends of the earth, represented by the robe.

The sacred robes of the High Priest are rich in symbolism. One such symbol is that the names of the children of Israel were engraved on the onyx stones mounted on the shoulder pieces of the ephod, the ancestor of our present-day chasuble: six on the stone of the right shoulder piece and six on that of the left (see Exod. 28:6–14). The names of the twelve tribes of Israel were also engraved on the breastplate (see Exod. 28:21). This means that the priest celebrates by carrying on his shoulders the people entrusted to his care and bearing their names written in his heart. When we put on our simple chasuble, it might well make us feel, upon our shoulders and in our hearts, the burdens and the faces of our faithful people, our saints and martyrs who are numerous in these times.

From the beauty of all these liturgical things, which is not so much about trappings and fine fabrics as it is about the glory of our God resplendent in his people, alive and strengthened, we turn now to a consideration of activity, action. The precious oil that anoints the head of Aaron does more than simply lend fragrance to his person; it overflows down to "the edges." The Lord will say this clearly: his anointing is meant for the poor, prisoners, and the sick, for those who are sorrowing and alone. My dear brothers, the ointment is not intended just to make us fragrant, much less to be kept in a jar, for then it would become rancid . . . and the heart bitter.

A good priest can be recognized by the way his people are anointed: this is a clear proof. When our people are anointed with the oil of gladness, it is obvious: for example, when they leave Mass looking as if they have heard good news. Our people like to hear the Gospel preached with "unction"; they like it when the Gospel we preach touches their daily lives, when it runs down like the oil of Aaron to the edges of reality, when it brings light to moments of extreme darkness, to the "outskirts" where people of faith are most exposed to the onslaught of those who want to tear down their faith. People thank us because they feel that we have prayed over the realities of their everyday lives—their troubles, their joys, their burdens, and their hopes. And when they feel that the fragrance of the Anointed One, of Christ, has come to them through us, they feel encouraged to entrust to us everything they want to bring before the Lord: "Pray for me, Father, because I have this problem," "Bless me Father," "Pray for me"—these words are the sign that the anointing has flowed down to the edges of the robe, for it has turned into a prayer of supplication, the supplication of the People of God. When we have this relationship with God and with his people, and grace passes through us, then we are priests, mediators between God and the people. What I want to emphasize is that we need constantly to stir up God's grace and perceive in every request, even those requests that are inconvenient and at times purely material or downright banal—but only apparently so—the desire of our people to be anointed with fragrant oil, since they know that we have it.

[We need] to perceive and to sense, even as the Lord sensed the hope-filled anguish of the woman suffering from hemorrhages when she touched the hem of his garment. At that moment, Jesus, surrounded by people on every side, embodies all the beauty of Aaron vested in priestly raiment, with the oil running down upon his robes. It is a hidden beauty, one that shines forth only for those faith-filled eyes of the woman troubled with an issue of blood. But not even the disciples—future priests—see or understand; on the "existential outskirts" they see only what is on the surface: the crowd pressing in on Jesus from all sides (see Luke 8:42). The Lord, however, feels the power of the divine anointing, which runs down to the edge of his cloak.

We need to "go out," then, in order to experience our own anointing, its power and its redemptive efficacy: to the "outskirts" where there is suffering, bloodshed, blindness that longs for sight, and prisoners in thrall to many evil masters. It is not in soul-searching or constant introspection that we encounter the Lord: self-help courses can be useful in life, but to live our priestly life going from one course to another, from one method to another, leads us to become Pelagians and to minimize the power of grace, which comes alive and flourishes to the extent that we, in faith, go out and give ourselves and the Gospel to others, giving what little ointment we have to those who have nothing, nothing at all.

The priest who seldom goes out of himself, who anoints little—I won't say "not at all" because, thank God, the people take the oil from us anyway—misses out on the best of our people, on what can stir the depths of his priestly heart. Those who do not go out of themselves, instead of being mediators, gradually become intermediaries, managers. We know the difference: the intermediary, the manager, "has already received his reward," and because he doesn't put his own skin and his own heart on the line, he never hears a warm, heartfelt word of thanks. This is precisely the reason for the

Those priests who do not go out of themselves, instead of being mediators, gradually become intermediaries, managers.

dissatisfaction of some, who end up sad—sad priests—in some sense becoming collectors of antiques or novelties, instead of being shepherds living with "the odor of the sheep." This I ask you: be shepherds, with the "odor of the sheep," make it real, as shepherds among your flock, fishers of people. True enough, the so-called crisis of priestly identity threatens us all and adds to the broader cultural crisis; but if we can resist its onslaught, we will be able to go out in the name of the Lord and cast our nets. It is not a bad thing that reality itself forces us to "put out into the deep," where what we are by grace is clearly seen as pure grace, out into the deep of the contemporary world, where the only thing that counts is "unction"—not function—and the nets that overflow with fish are those cast solely in the name of the One in whom we have put our trust: Jesus.

PART SEVEN

The Choice of the Last

25

To the Outskirts of Existence

Address to the Lay Movements on Pentecost Vigil, 18 May 2013

The Church must step outside herself. To go where? To the outskirts of existence, whatever they may be, but she must step out. Jesus tells us, "Go into all the world! Go! Preach! Bear witness to the Gospel!" (see Mark 16:15). But what happens if we step outside ourselves? The same as can happen to anyone who comes out of the house and onto the street: an accident. But I tell you, I far prefer a Church that has had a few accidents to a Church that has fallen sick from being closed. Go out, go out!

Think of what the book of Revelation says as well. It says something beautiful: that Jesus stands at the door and knocks, knocks to be let into our heart (see Rev. 3:20). This is the meaning of the book of Revelation. But ask yourselves this question: how often is Jesus inside and knocking at the door to be let out, to come out?

> *So often we are locked into ephemeral structures that serve solely to make us slaves and not free children of God.*

And we do not let him out because of our own need for security, because so often we are locked into ephemeral structures that serve solely to make us slaves and not free children of God.

In this "stepping out" it is important to be ready for encounter. For me this word is very important. Encounter with others. Why? Because faith is an encounter with Jesus, and we must do what Jesus does: encounter others. We live in a culture of conflict, a culture of fragmentation, a culture in which I throw away what is of no use to me, a culture of waste. Yet on this point, I ask you to think—and it is part of the crisis—of the elderly, who are the wisdom of a people; think of the children . . . the culture of waste! However, we must go out to meet them, and with our faith we must create a "culture of encounter," a culture of friendship, a culture in which we find brothers and sisters, in which we can also speak with those who think differently, as well as those who hold other beliefs, who do not have the same faith. They all have something in common with us: they are images of God; they are children of God. [We must be] going out to meet everyone, without losing sight of our own position.

There is another important point: encountering the poor. If we step outside ourselves, we find poverty. Today—it sickens the heart to say so—the discovery of a tramp who has died of the cold is not news. Today what counts as news is, maybe, a scandal. A scandal—ah, that is news! Today, the thought that a great many children do not have food to eat is not news. This is serious; this is serious! We cannot put up with this! Yet that is how things are.

We cannot become starched Christians, those overeducated Christians who speak of theological matters as they calmly sip their tea. No! We must become courageous Christians and go in search of the people who are the very flesh of Christ—those who are the flesh of Christ! When I go to hear confessions—I still can't, because to go out to hear confessions . . . from here it's impossible to go out, but that's another problem—when I *used* to go to hear confessions in my previous diocese, people would come to me, and I would always ask them: "Do you give alms?" "Yes, Father!" "Very good." And I would ask them two further questions: "Tell me, when you give alms, do you look the person in the eye?" "Oh, I don't know. I haven't really thought about it." The second question: "And when you give alms, do you touch the hand of the person you are giving them to, or do you toss the coin at him or her?" This is the [issue]: the flesh of Christ, touching the flesh of Christ, taking upon ourselves this suffering for the poor.

Poverty for us Christians is not a sociological, philosophical, or cultural category, no. It is theological. I might say this is the first category, because our God, the Son of God, abased himself, he made himself poor to walk along the road with us. This is our poverty: the poverty of the flesh of Christ, the poverty that brought the Son of God to us through his incarnation. A poor Church for the poor begins by reaching out to the flesh of Christ. If we reach out to the flesh of Christ, we begin to understand something, to understand this poverty, the Lord's poverty.

26

Hospitality and Service

Address to the Missionaries of the Homeless Shelter Dono di Maria,
21 May 2013

When we say "home," we mean a place of hospitality, a dwelling, a pleasant human environment where one stays readily, finds oneself, feels inserted into a territory, a community. Yet more profoundly, *home* is a word with a typically familiar flavor, which recalls warmth, affection, and the love that can be felt in a family. Hence the home represents the most precious human treasures: encounter, relations among people who are different in age, culture, and history, but who live together and help one another to grow. For this reason, the home is a crucial place in life, where life grows and can be fulfilled, because it is a place in which every person learns to receive love and to give love. This is "home." And this is what *this* home has tried to be for twenty-five years! On the border between the Vatican and Italy, it is a strong appeal to us all—to the Church, to the city of Rome—to be more and more of a family, a "home" open to hospitality, care, and brotherhood.

There is then a second very important word: *gift*, which qualifies this home and describes its typical identity. It is a home, in fact, that is characterized by gift, by mutual gift. What do I mean? I wish to say that this home gives hospitality—material and spiritual sustenance to you, dear guests, who have come from different parts of the world. But you are also a gift for this home and for the Church. You tell us that to love God and neighbor is not something abstract, but profoundly concrete: it means seeing in every person the face of the Lord to be served, and to serve him concretely. And you are, dear brothers and sisters, the face of Jesus. Thank you! To all those who work in this place, you give the possibility to serve Jesus in those who are in difficulty, who are in need of help.

This home, then, is a luminous transparency of the charity of God, who is a good and merciful Father to all. Open hospitality is lived here, without distinctions of nationality or religion, according to the teaching of Jesus: "You received without pay, give without pay" (Matt. 10:8). We must recover the whole sense of gift, of gratuitousness, of solidarity. Rampant capitalism has taught the logic of profit at all costs, of giving to get, of exploitation without looking at the person . . . and we see the results in the crisis we are experiencing! This home is a place that teaches charity; it is a "school" of charity, which instructs me to go and encounter every person, not for profit, but for love.

> *This home is a place that teaches charity; it is a "school" of charity, which instructs me to go and encounter every person, not for profit, but for love.*

27

Refugees and Those Uprooted from Life

Address to the Participants in the Plenary of the Pontifical Council
for the Pastoral Care of Migrants and Itinerant People,
24 May 2013

The Church is mother, and her motherly attention is expressed with special tenderness and closeness to those who are obliged to flee their own country and exist between rootlessness and integration. This tension destroys people. Christian compassion—this "suffering with" compassion—is expressed first of all in the commitment to obtain knowledge of the events that force people to leave their homeland, and where necessary, to give voice to those who cannot manage to make their cry of distress and oppression heard. By doing this you also carry out an important task in sensitizing Christian communities to the multitudes of their brothers and sisters scarred by wounds that mark their existence: violence, abuse, the distance from family love, traumatic events, flight from home, and uncertainty about the future in refugee camps. These are all dehumanizing elements and must spur every Christian and the whole community to practical concern.

Today, however, dear friends, I would like to ask you all to see a ray of hope as well in the eyes and hearts of refugees and of those who have been forcibly displaced—a hope that is expressed in expectations for the future, in the desire for friendship, in the wish to participate in the host society through learning the language, access to employment, and the education of children.

I admire the courage of those who hope to be able gradually to resume a normal life, waiting for joy and love to return to brighten their existence. We can and must all nourish this hope!

Above all I ask leaders and legislators and the entire international community to confront the reality of those who have been displaced by force, with effective projects and new approaches in order to protect their dignity, to improve the quality of their life, and to face the challenges that are emerging from modern forms of persecution, oppression, and slavery. They are human people—I stress this—who are appealing for solidarity and assistance, who need urgent action but, also and above all, understanding and kindness. God is good; let us imitate God.

[The condition of displaced peoples] cannot leave us indifferent. Moreover, as Church, we should remember that in tending the wounds of refugees, evacuees, and the victims of trafficking, we are putting into practice the commandment of love that Jesus bequeathed to us when he identified with the foreigner, with those who are suffering, with all the innocent victims of violence and exploitation. We should reread more often chapter 25 of the Gospel according to Matthew in which he speaks of the Last Judgment (see Matt. 25:31–46).

And here I would also like to remind you of the attention that every pastor and Christian community must pay to the journey of faith of Christian refugees and Christians uprooted from their situations by force, as well as of Christian emigrants. These people need special pastoral care that respects their traditions and accompanies them to harmonious integration into the ecclesial situations in which they find themselves. May our Christian communities really be places of hospitality, listening, and communion!

These people need special pastoral care that respects their traditions and accompanies them to harmonious integration into the ecclesial situations in which they find themselves.

28

A Culture of Solidarity

Address at the Astalli Centre, the Jesuit Refugee Service in Rome,
10 September 2013

What does serving mean? It means giving an attentive welcome to a person who arrives. It means bending over those in need and stretching out a hand to them, without calculation, without fear, but with tenderness and understanding, just as Jesus knelt to wash the apostles' feet. Serving means working beside the neediest of people, establishing with them first and foremost human relationships of closeness and bonds of solidarity. *Solidarity*, this word that frightens the developed world. People try to avoid saying it. *Solidarity* to them is almost a bad word. But it is our word! Serving means recognizing and accepting requests for justice and hope, and seeking roads together, real paths that lead to liberation.

The poor are also the privileged teachers of our knowledge of God; their frailty and simplicity unmask our selfishness, our false security, and our claim to be self-sufficient. The poor guide us to experience God's closeness and tenderness, to receive his love in our life, his mercy as the Father who cares for us, for all of us, with discretion and patient trust.

From this place of welcome, encounter, and service, I would therefore like to launch a question to everyone, to all the people who live here, in this Diocese of Rome: Ask yourself, Do I bend down over someone in difficulty, or am I afraid of getting my hands dirty? Am I closed in on myself and my possessions, or am I aware of those in need of help? Do I serve only myself, or am I able to serve others, like Christ who came to serve even to the point of giving up his life? Do I look in the eye those who are asking for justice, or do I turn my gaze aside to avoid looking them in the eye?

A second word: *accompanying*. In recent years the Astalli Centre has progressed. At the outset it offered services of basic hospitality: a soup kitchen, a place to sleep, legal assistance. It then learned to accompany people in their search for a job and to fit into society. Then it also proposed cultural activities so as to contribute to increasing a culture of acceptance, a culture of encounter and of solidarity, starting with the safeguard of human rights.

Accompanying on its own is not enough. It is not enough to offer someone a sandwich unless it is accompanied by the possibility of learning how to stand on one's own two feet. Charity that leaves the poor person as he or she is, is not sufficient. True mercy, the mercy God gives to us and teaches us, demands justice; it demands that the poor find the way to be poor no longer. It asks—and it asks us, the Church, us, the city of Rome, it asks the institutions—to ensure that no one ever again stand in need of a soup kitchen, of makeshift lodgings, of a service of legal assistance in order to have their legitimate right recognized to live and to work, to be fully a person. Adam said, "It is our duty as refugees to do our best to be integrated in Italy." And this is a right: integration! And Carol said, "Syrians in Europe feel the great responsibility not to be a burden. We want to feel we are an active part of a new society." This is a right too! So this responsibility is the ethical basis, it is the power to build together. I wonder: do we accompany people in this process?

> *True mercy, the mercy God gives to us and teaches us, demands justice; it demands that the poor find the way to be poor no longer.*

The third word: *defending*. Serving and accompanying also means defending; it means taking the side of the weakest. How often do we raise our voice to defend our own rights, but how often we are indifferent to the rights of others! How many times we don't know or don't want to give voice to the voice of those—like you—who have suffered and are suffering, of those who have seen their own rights trampled upon, of those who have experienced so much violence that it has even stifled their desire to have justice done!

It is important for the whole Church that welcoming the poor and promoting justice not be entrusted solely to "experts" but become a focus of all pastoral care, of the formation of future priests and religious, and of the ordinary work of all parishes, movements, and ecclesial groups. In particular—this is important and I say it from my heart—I would also like to ask religious institutes to interpret seriously and with responsibility this sign of the times. The Lord calls us to live with greater courage, generosity, and hospitality in communities, in houses, and in empty convents. Dear men and women religious, your empty convents are not useful to the Church if they are turned into hotels that earn money. The empty convents do not belong to you; they are for the flesh of Christ, which is what refugees are. The Lord calls us to live with greater courage and generosity, and to accept them in communities, houses, and empty convents. This of course is not something simple; it requires a criterion and responsibility, but also courage. We do a great deal, but perhaps we are called to do more, firmly accepting and sharing with those whom Providence has given us to serve.

PART EIGHT

Demolishing the Idols

29

The Logic of Power and Violence

Homily at the Vigil of Prayer for Peace, 7 September 2013

Isn't the world we want a world of harmony and peace—in ourselves, in our relations with others, in families, in cities, *in* and *between* nations? And does not true freedom mean choosing ways in this world that lead to the good of all and are guided by love?

But then we wonder: is this the world in which we are living? Creation retains its beauty, which fills us with awe, and it remains a good work. But there is also "violence, division, disagreement, war." This occurs when human beings, the summit of creation, stop contemplating beauty and goodness, and withdraw into their own selfishness.

When we think only of ourselves and our own interests and place ourselves in the center, when we permit ourselves to be captivated by the idols of dominion and power, when we put ourselves in God's place, then all relationships are broken and everything is ruined; then the door opens to violence, indifference, and conflict. This is precisely what the passage in the book of Genesis seeks to teach us in the story of the Fall: the man enters into conflict with himself, he realizes that he is naked, and he hides himself because he is afraid (see Gen. 3:10). He is afraid of God's glance; he accuses the woman, she who is flesh of his flesh (see Gen. 3:12); he breaks harmony with creation, and he begins to raise his hand against his brother to kill him. Can we say that from harmony he passes to "disharmony"? No, there is no such thing

111

as disharmony; there is either harmony or we fall into chaos, where there is violence, argument, conflict, fear . . .

It is exactly in this chaos that God asks the man's conscience, "Where is Abel your brother?" and Cain responds, "I do not know; am I my brother's keeper?" (Gen. 4:9). We too are asked this question; it would be good for us to ask ourselves as well: am I really my brother's keeper? Yes, you are your brother's keeper! To be human means to care for one another! But when harmony is broken, a metamorphosis occurs: the brother who is to be cared for and loved becomes an adversary to fight and kill. What violence occurs at that moment, how many conflicts, how many wars have marked our history! We need only look at the suffering of so many brothers and sisters. This is not a question of coincidence, but the truth: we bring about the rebirth of Cain in every act of violence and in every war. All of us!

And even today we continue this history of conflict between people, even today we raise our hands against our brother or sister. Even today we let ourselves be guided by idols, by selfishness, by our own interests, and this attitude persists. We have perfected our weapons, our conscience has fallen asleep, and we have sharpened our ideas to justify ourselves.

> *We have perfected our weapons, our conscience has fallen asleep, and we have sharpened our ideas to justify ourselves.*

As if it were normal, we continue to sow destruction, pain, death! Violence and war lead only to death; they speak of death! Violence and war are the language of death!

30

The Cult of the God of Money

General Audience, 5 June 2013

It is no longer the person who commands, but money, money, cash commands. And God our Father gave us the task of protecting the earth—not for money, but for ourselves, for men and women. We have this task! Nevertheless men and women are sacrificed to the idols of profit and consumption: it is the "culture of waste." If a computer breaks, it is a tragedy; but poverty, the needs and dramas of so many people, end up being considered normal. If on a winter's night—here on the Via Ottaviano, for example—someone dies, that is not news. If there are children in so many parts of the world who have nothing to eat, that is not news; it seems normal. It cannot be so! And yet these things enter into normality: that some homeless people should freeze to death on the street—this doesn't make news. On the contrary, when the stock market drops ten points in some cities, it constitutes a tragedy. Someone who dies is not news, but lowering income by ten points is a tragedy! In this way people are thrown aside as if they were trash.

This "culture of waste" tends to become a common mentality that infects everyone. Human life, the person, is no longer seen as a primary value to be respected and safeguarded, especially if that person is poor or disabled or not yet useful, like the unborn child, or is no longer of any use, like the elderly person. This

Let us remember well, however, that whenever food is thrown out, it is as if it were stolen from the table of the poor, from the hungry!

culture of waste has also made us insensitive to wasting and throwing out excess foodstuffs, which is especially condemnable when, in every part of the world, unfortunately, many individuals and families suffer hunger and malnutrition. There was a time when our grandparents were very careful not to throw away any leftover food. Consumerism has induced us to be accustomed to excess and to the daily waste of food, whose value, which goes far beyond mere financial parameters, we are no longer able to judge correctly. Let us remember well, however, that whenever food is thrown out, it is as if it were stolen from the table of the poor, from the hungry! I ask everyone to reflect on the problem of the loss and waste of food, to identify ways and approaches that, by seriously dealing with this problem, convey solidarity and sharing with the underprivileged.

31

The Leprosy of Careerism

Address to the Community of the Pontifical Ecclesiastical Academy,
6 June 2013

What does having inner freedom mean?

First of all it means being free from personal projects. Free from some of the tangible ways in which, perhaps, you may once have conceived of living your priesthood: from the possibility of planning your future or from the prospect of staying for any length of time in a place of "your own" pastoral action. It means, in a certain way, making yourself free also with regard to the culture and mind-set from which you come. This is not in order to forget it or even less to deny it, but rather to open yourselves in the charity of understanding different cultures and meeting people who belong to worlds far distant from your own.

Above all, inner freedom means being alert to ensure that you keep free of the ambitions or personal aims that can cause the Church great

> *Careerism is a form of leprosy, a leprosy.*

harm. You must be careful not to make either your own fulfillment or the recognition you might receive both inside and outside the ecclesial community a constant priority. Rather, your priority should be the loftier good of the Gospel cause and the accomplishment of the mission that will be entrusted to you. And I think this being free from ambitions or personal goals is important—it is *important*. Careerism is a form of leprosy, a leprosy. No careerism, please. For this reason you must be prepared to integrate all your own views of the Church—however legitimate they may be—and every personal idea or opinion, into the horizon of Peter's gaze. You must integrate them into his specific mission at the service of the communion and unity of Christ's flock, of his pastoral charity that embraces the whole world and wishes to be present, partly through the action of the papal representations, especially in those all-too-often forsaken places where the needs of the Church and of humanity are greater.

32

Undressing the Spirit of the World

Speech in the Room of Renunciation in the Archbishop's Residence,
4 October 2013

During my visit to Assisi for St. Francis's day, the newspapers and media were stirring up fantasies. "The Pope is going to strip the Church there!" "What will he strip from the Church?" "He is going to strip bishops and cardinals of their vestments; then he will divest himself." This is, indeed, a good occasion to invite the Church to divest herself. But we are all the Church! All of us! Beginning with the newly baptized, we are all Church, and we must all follow the path of Jesus, who himself took the road of renunciation. He became a servant, one who serves; he chose to be humiliated even to the cross. And if we want to be Christians, then there is no other way.

But can't we make Christianity a little more human, they say, without the cross, without Jesus, without renunciation? In this way we would become like Christians in a pastry shop, saying: what beautiful cakes, what beautiful sweets! Truly beautiful, but not really Christians! Someone could ask, Of what must the Church divest herself? Today she must strip herself of a very grave danger, which threatens every person in the Church, everyone: the danger of worldliness. The Christian cannot coexist with the spirit of the world, with the worldliness that leads us to vanity, to arrogance, to pride. And this is an idol; it is not God. It is an idol! And idolatry is the gravest of sins!

When the media speaks about the Church, they believe the Church is made up of priests, sisters, bishops, cardinals, and the pope. But we are all

117

the Church, as I said. And we all must strip ourselves of this worldliness: the spirit opposing the spirit of the Beatitudes, the spirit opposing the spirit of Jesus. Worldliness hurts us. It is so very sad to find a worldly Christian who is sure—according to him or her—of that security that the faith gives and of the security that the world provides. You cannot be on both sides. The Church—all of us—must strip herself of the worldliness that leads to vanity, to pride, that is idolatry.

Jesus himself told us: "You cannot serve two masters: either you serve God or you serve mammon" (see Matt. 6:24). In mammon itself there is this worldly spirit; money, vanity, pride, that path . . . We cannot take it . . . It is sad to erase with one hand what we write with the other.

Jesus made himself a servant for our sake, and the spirit of the world has nothing to do with this.

The Gospel is the Gospel! God is one! And Jesus made himself a servant for our sake, and the spirit of the world has nothing to do with this. Today I am here with you. Many of you have been stripped by this callous world that offers no work, no help. To this world it doesn't matter that there are children dying of hunger; it doesn't matter if many families have nothing to eat, do not have the dignity of bringing bread home; it doesn't matter that many people are forced to flee slavery, hunger, and flee in search of freedom. With how much pain, how often don't we see that they meet death, as in Lampedusa: today is a day of tears! The spirit of the world causes these things. It is unthinkable that a Christian—a true Christian—be it a priest, a sister, a bishop, a cardinal, or a pope, would want to go down this path of worldliness, which is a homicidal attitude. Spiritual worldliness kills! It kills the soul! It kills the person! It kills the Church!

PART NINE

The Culture of Good

33

Free to Choose Good

Address to the Students of the Jesuit Schools, 7 June 2013

I would like first of all to tell you something that has to do with St. Ignatius of Loyola, our founder. In the autumn of 1537, on his way to Rome with a group of his first companions, he wondered, *If people ask us who we are, how should we answer?* The answer came spontaneously: We shall say that we are the "Society of Jesus" (*Fontes narrativi Societatis Iesu*, vol. 1, pp. 320–22). This demanding name intends to suggest a relationship of very close friendship and of total affection for Jesus, in whose footsteps they wanted to follow. Why have I told you about this event? Because St. Ignatius and his companions had realized that Jesus was teaching them how to live well, how to live a life that had profound meaning, that imparted enthusiasm, joy, and hope. They had understood that Jesus is a great teacher of life and a model of life, and that he was not only teaching them but also inviting them to follow him on this path.

Dear young people, if I were to ask you now why you go to school, what would you answer me? There would probably be a whole range of replies, according to the sensibility of each person. Yet I think that they could all be summed up together by saying that school is one of the educational environments in which we develop through learning how to live, how to become grown-up, mature men and women who can travel, who can follow the road of life. How does school help you grow? It helps you not only by developing your intelligence but also by an integral formation of all the aspects of your personality.

In following what St. Ignatius teaches us, the main element at school is to learn to be magnanimous. Magnanimity: this virtue of the great and the small (*Non coerceri maximo contineri minimo, divinum est*), which always makes us look at the horizon. What does being magnanimous mean? It means having a great heart, having greatness of mind; it means having great ideals, the wish to do great things in response to what God asks of us. [It means also] to do well the routine . . . daily actions, tasks, meetings with people—doing the little everyday things with a great heart open to God and to others. It is therefore important to cultivate human formation with a view to magnanimity. School not only broadens your intellectual dimension but also your human one. And I think that Jesuit schools take special care to develop human virtues: loyalty, respect, faithfulness, and dedication.

I would like to reflect on two fundamental values: freedom and service. First of all: be free people! What do I mean? Perhaps it is thought that freedom means doing everything one likes, or seeing how far one can go by trying drunkenness and overcoming boredom. This is not freedom. Freedom means being able to think about what we do, being able to assess what is good

> *Being free always to choose goodness is demanding, but it will make you into people with backbone who can face life, people with courage and patience.*

and what is bad; these are the types of conduct that lead to development; it means always opting for the good. Let us be free for goodness. And in this do not be afraid to go against the tide, even if it is not easy! Being free always to choose goodness is demanding, but it will make you into people with backbone who can face life, people with courage and patience (*parrhesia* and *ypomoné*).

The second word is *service*. In your schools you take part in various activities that accustom you to not retreating into yourselves or into your own small world, but rather to being open to others, especially the poorest and neediest. They accustom you to working hard to improve the world in which we live. Be men and women with others and for others, true champions at the service of others.

In order to be magnanimous with inner freedom and a spirit of service, spiritual formation is necessary. Dear young people, love Jesus Christ more and more! Our life is a response to his call, and you will be happy and will build your life well if you can answer this call. May you feel the Lord's presence in your life. He is close to each one of you as a companion, as a friend who knows how to help and understand you, who encourages you in difficult times and never abandons you. In prayer, in conversation with him, and in reading the Bible, you will discover that he is truly close. You will also learn to read God's signs in your life. He always speaks to us, also through the events of our time and our daily life; it is up to us to listen to him.

34

The Hunger for Dignity

Address to the Community of Varginha, 25 July 2013

Especially the humblest people can offer the world a valuable lesson in solidarity. This word *solidarity* is too often forgotten or silenced, because it makes us uncomfortable. It almost seems like a bad word . . . *solidarity*. I would like to make an appeal to those in possession of greater resources, to public authorities and to all people of goodwill who are working for social justice: never tire of working for a more just world, marked by greater solidarity! No one can remain insensitive to the inequalities that persist in the world! Everybody, according to his or her particular opportunities and responsibilities, should be able to make a personal contribution to putting an end to so many social injustices. The culture of selfishness and individualism that often prevails in our society is not—I repeat, *not*—what builds up and leads to a more habitable world: rather, it is the culture of solidarity that does so. In the culture of solidarity we see others not as rivals or statistics, but as brothers and sisters. And we are all brothers and sisters!

I would like to encourage the efforts that Brazilian society is making to integrate all its members, including those who suffer most and are in greatest need, through the fight against hunger and deprivation. No amount of "peace-building" will be able to last, nor will harmony and happiness be attained, in a society that ignores, pushes to the margins, or excludes a part of itself. A society of that kind simply impoverishes itself; it loses something essential. We must never, never allow the throwaway culture to enter our hearts! We must never allow the throwaway culture to enter our hearts, because we are brothers and sisters. No one is disposable! Let us always remember this: only when we are able to share do we become truly rich; everything that is shared is multiplied! Think of the multiplication of the loaves by Jesus! The measure of the greatness of a society is found in the way it treats those most in need, those who have nothing apart from their poverty!

I would also like to tell you that the Church, the "advocate of justice and defender of the poor in the face of intolerable social and economic inequalities which cry to heaven" (Aparecida Document, para. 395), wishes to offer her support for every initiative that can signify genuine development for every person and for the whole

> But there is also a deeper hunger, the hunger for a happiness that only God can satisfy, the hunger for dignity.

person. Dear friends, it is certainly necessary to give bread to the hungry—this is an act of justice. But there is also a deeper hunger, the hunger for a happiness that only God can satisfy, the hunger for dignity. There is neither real promotion of the common good nor real human development when there is ignorance of the fundamental pillars that govern a nation, its nonmaterial goods: *life*, which is a gift of God, a value always to be protected and promoted; the *family*, the foundation of coexistence and a remedy against social fragmentation; *integral education*, which cannot be reduced to the mere transmission of information for purposes of generating profit; *health*, which must seek the integral well-being of the person, including the spiritual dimension, essential for human balance and healthy coexistence; *security*, in the conviction that violence can be overcome only by changing human hearts.

I would like to add one final point. Here, as in the whole of Brazil, there are many young people. You young people, my dear young friends, you have a particular sensitivity toward injustice, but you are often disappointed by facts that speak of corruption on the part of people who put their own interests before the common good. To you and to all, I repeat: never yield to discouragement, do not lose trust, do not allow your hope to be extinguished. Situations can change; people can change. Be the first to seek to bring good.

35

The Commitment to Peace

Address to the Participants in the International Meeting for Peace Sponsored by the Community of Sant'Egidio, 30 September 2013

As leaders of different religions we can do a lot. Peace is the responsibility of everyone—to pray for peace, to work for peace! A religious *leader* is always a man or woman of peace, for the commandment of peace is inscribed in the depths of the religious traditions that we represent. But what can we do? Your annual meeting suggests the way forward: the courage of dialogue. This courage, this dialogue, gives us hope. It has nothing to do with optimism; it is entirely different. Hope!

In the world, in society, there is little peace because dialogue is missing; we find it difficult to go beyond the narrow horizon of our own interests in order to open ourselves to a true and sincere comparison. Peace requires a persistent, patient, strong, intelligent dialogue by which

> *Peace requires a persistent, patient, strong, intelligent dialogue by which nothing is lost.*

nothing is lost. Dialogue can overcome war. Dialogue can bring people of different generations who often ignore one another to live together; it makes citizens of different ethnic backgrounds and of different beliefs coexist. Dialogue is the way of peace. For dialogue fosters understanding, harmony, concord, and peace. For this reason, it is vital that it grow and expand between people of every condition and belief, like a net of peace that protects the world and especially protects the weakest members.

As religious *leaders*, we are called to be true "people of dialogue," to cooperate in building peace not as intermediaries but as authentic mediators. Intermediaries seek to give everyone a discount ultimately in order to gain something for themselves. However, the mediator is one who retains nothing for himself but rather spends himself generously until he is consumed, knowing that the only gain is peace. Each one of us is called to be an artisan of peace, by uniting and not dividing, by extinguishing hatred and not holding on to it, by opening paths to dialogue and not by constructing new walls! Let us dialogue and meet one another in order to establish a culture of dialogue in the world, a culture of encounter.

36

For a New Solidarity

Address to the Centesimus Annus Pro Pontifice Foundation,
25 May 2013

What does "rethinking solidarity" mean? It does not of course mean calling into question the recent magisterium, which, on the contrary, is increasingly showing how farsighted and up-to-date it is. Rather . . . it seems to me to mean two things. First of all, this rethinking combines the magisterium with social and economic development because it is constant and rapid, revealing ever new aspects. Second, "rethinking" means deepening knowledge, reflecting further to enhance all the fruitfulness of a value—solidarity in this case—which draws in depth from the Gospel, that is, from Jesus Christ, and so as such contains an inexhaustible potential.

Today's economic and social crisis makes this rethinking ever more urgent and highlights even more clearly the truth and timeliness of affirmations of the social magisterium such as the one we read in *Laborem exercens*: "As we view the whole human family . . . we cannot fail to be struck by a disconcerting fact of immense proportions: the fact that, while conspicuous natural resources remain unused, there are huge numbers of people who are unemployed or underemployed and countless multitudes of people suffering from hunger. This is a fact that without any doubt demonstrates that . . . there is something wrong" (no. 18). Unemployment—the lack or loss of work—is a phenomenon that is spreading like an oil slick in vast areas of the West and is alarmingly widening the boundaries of poverty. Moreover, there is no worse material poverty, I am keen to stress, than the poverty that prevents people from earning their bread and deprives them of the dignity of work. Well, this "something wrong" no longer relates only to the South of the world but also to the entire planet. Hence the need to rethink solidarity no longer as simply assistance for the poorest, but as a global rethinking of the whole system, as a quest for ways to reform it and correct it in a way consistent with the fundamental rights of all human beings.

It is essential to restore to this word *solidarity*, viewed askance by the world of economics—as if it were a bad word—the social citizenship that it deserves. Solidarity is not an additional attitude; it is not a form of social almsgiving but, rather, a social value, and it asks us for its citizenship.

The current crisis is not only economic and financial but is rooted in an ethical and anthropological crisis. Concern with the idols of power, profit, and money, rather than with the value of the human person, has become a basic norm for functioning and a crucial criterion for organization. We have forgotten and are still forgetting that over and above business, logic, and the parameters of the market is the human being; and that "something" is men and women, inasmuch as they are human beings by virtue of their profound dignity: to offer them the possibility of living a dignified life and of actively participating in the common good.

> *Concern with the idols of power, profit, and money, rather than with the value of the human person, has become a basic norm for functioning and a crucial criterion for organization.*

PART TEN

Mary, Mother of Evangelization

37

Her Example

Address at the End of the Marian Month of May, 31 May 2013

Three words sum up Mary's attitude: listening, decision, and action. They are words that point out a way for us too as we face what the Lord asks of us in life. Listening, decision, action.

1. *Listening.* What gave rise to Mary's act of going to visit her relative Elizabeth? A word of God's angel: "Elizabeth in her old age has also conceived a son" (Luke 1:36). Mary knew how to listen to God. Be careful: it was not merely *hearing*, a superficial word, but it was *listening*, which consists of attention, acceptance, and availability to God. It was not in the distracted way with which we sometimes face the Lord or others: we hear their words, but we do not really listen. Mary is attentive to God. She listens to God.

However, Mary also listens to the events—that is, she interprets the events of her life; she is attentive to reality itself and does not stop on the surface but goes to the depths to grasp its meaning. Her kinswoman Elizabeth, who is already elderly, is expecting a child; this is the event. But Mary is attentive to the meaning. She can understand it: "with God nothing will be impossible" (Luke 1:37).

This is also true in our life: listening to God who speaks to us, and listening also to daily reality, paying attention to people, to events, because the Lord is at the door of our life and knocks in many ways; he puts signs on our path, and he gives us the ability to see them. Mary is the mother of listening, of attentive listening to God and of equally attentive listening to the events of life.

2. The second word: *decision*. Mary did not live "with haste," with breathlessness, but, as St. Luke emphasizes, she "kept all these things, pondering them in her heart" (see Luke 2:19, 51). Moreover, at the crucial moment of the angel's annunciation, she also asks, "How shall this be?" (Luke 1:34). Yet she does not stop at

> *Mary does not let herself be dragged along by events; she does not avoid the effort of making a decision.*

the moment of reflection either. She goes a step further: she decides. She does not live in haste but "goes with haste" only when necessary. Mary does not let herself be dragged along by events; she does not avoid the effort of making a decision. And this happens both in the fundamental decision that was to change her life—"I am the handmaid of the Lord . . ." (see Luke 1:38)—and in her daily decisions, routine but also full of meaning. The episode of the wedding of Cana springs to my mind (see John 2:1–11): here too one sees the realism, humanity, and practicality of Mary, who is attentive to events, to problems. She sees and understands the difficulty of the young married couple at whose wedding feast the wine runs out; she thinks about it; she knows that Jesus can do something and decides to address her Son so that he may intervene: "they have no more wine" (John 2:3). She decides.

It is difficult in life to make decisions. We often tend to put them off, to let others decide instead; we frequently prefer to let ourselves be dragged along by events, to follow the current fashion. At times we know what we ought to do, but we do not have the courage to do it, or it seems to us too difficult because it means swimming against the tide. In the Annunciation, in the Visitation, and at the wedding of Cana, Mary goes against the tide. Mary goes against the tide; she listens to God, she reflects and seeks to understand reality, and she decides to entrust herself totally to God. Although she is with child, she decides to visit her elderly relative, and [years later] she decides to entrust herself to her Son with insistence so as to preserve the joy of the wedding feast.

3. The third word: *action*. Mary set out on a journey and "went with haste" (see Luke 1:39). Last Sunday I underlined Mary's way of acting: in spite of the difficulties, the criticism she would have met with because of her decision to go, nothing could stop her. And here she leaves "with haste." In prayer, before God who speaks, in thinking and meditating on the facts of her life, Mary is not in a hurry: she does not let herself be swept away by the moment; she does not let herself be dragged along by events. However, when she has clearly understood what God is asking of her, what she has to do, she does not loiter, she does not delay, but she goes "with haste." St. Ambrose commented, "There is nothing slow about the Holy Spirit" (*Expos. Evang. sec. Lucam*, II, 19: *PL* 15, 1560). Mary's action was a consequence of her obedience to the angel's words but was combined with charity: she went to Elizabeth to make herself useful; and in going out of her home, of herself, for love, she takes with her the most precious thing she has: Jesus. She takes her Son.

We likewise sometimes stop at listening, at thinking about what we must do; we may even be clear about the decision we have to make, but we do not move on to action. And above all we do not put ourselves at stake by moving toward others "with haste" so as to bring them our help, our understanding, our love—to bring them, as Mary did, the most precious thing we have received, Jesus and his Gospel, with words, and above all with the tangible witness of what we do.

Mary, the woman of listening, of decision, of action.

38

Her Faith

Prayer for the Marian Day, 12 October 2013

We can ask: what was Mary's faith like?

1. The first aspect of her faith is this: Mary's faith unties the knot of sin (see *Lumen gentium*, 56). What does that mean? The Fathers of the Second Vatican Council took up a phrase of St. Irenaeus, who states that "the knot of Eve's disobedience was untied by the obedience of Mary; what the virgin Eve bound by her unbelief, the Virgin Mary loosened by her faith" (*Adversus haereses*, III, 22, 4).

The "knot" of disobedience, the "knot" of unbelief. When children disobey their parents, we can say that a little "knot" is created. This happens if the child acts with an awareness of what he or she is doing, especially if there is a lie involved. At that moment, children break trust with their parents. You know how frequently this happens! Then the relationship with their

> When we do concrete things that demonstrate our lack of trust in him—for that is what sin is—a kind of knot is created deep within us.

parents needs to be purified of this fault; the child has to ask forgiveness so that harmony and trust can be restored. Something of the same sort happens in our relationship with God. When we do not listen to him, when we do not follow his will, we do concrete things that demonstrate our lack of trust in him—for that is what sin is—and a kind of knot is created deep within us. These knots take away our peace and serenity. They are dangerous, since many knots can form a tangle that gets more and more painful and difficult to undo.

But we know one thing: nothing is impossible for God's mercy! Even the most tangled knots are loosened by his grace. And Mary, whose "yes" opened the door for God to undo the knot of the ancient disobedience, is the Mother who patiently and lovingly brings us to God, so that he can untangle the knots of our soul by his fatherly mercy. We all have some of these knots, and we can ask in our heart of hearts: what are the knots in my life? "Father, my knots cannot be undone!" It is a mistake to say anything of the sort! All the knots of our heart, every knot of our conscience, can be undone. Do I ask Mary to help me trust in God's mercy, to undo those knots, to change? She, as a woman of faith, will surely tell you, "Get up, go to the Lord: he understands you." And she leads us by the hand as a mother, our Mother, to the embrace of our Father, the Father of mercies.

2. A second aspect is that Mary's faith gave human flesh to Jesus. As the Second Vatican Council says: "Through her faith and obedience, she gave birth on earth to the very Son of the Father, without knowing man but by the overshadowing of the Holy Spirit" (*Lumen gentium*, no. 63). This was a point on which the Fathers of the Church greatly insisted: Mary first conceived Jesus in faith and then in the flesh, when she said yes to the message God gave her through the angel. What does this mean? It means that God did not want to become human by bypassing our freedom; he wanted to pass through Mary's free assent, through her "yes." He asked her, "Are you prepared to do this?" And she replied, "Yes."

But what took place most singularly in the Virgin Mary also takes place within us, spiritually, when we receive the word of God with a good and sincere heart and put it into practice. It is as if God takes flesh within us; he comes to dwell in us, for he dwells in all who love him and keep his word. It is not easy to understand this, but really, it is easy to feel it in our heart.

Do we think that Jesus' incarnation is simply a past event that has nothing to do with us personally? Believing in Jesus means giving him our flesh with the humility and courage of Mary, so that he can continue to dwell in our midst. It means giving him our hands, to caress the little ones and the poor; our feet, to go forth and meet

> *Believing in Jesus means giving him our flesh with the humility and courage of Mary, so that he can continue to dwell in our midst.*

our brothers and sisters; our arms, to hold up the weak and to work in the Lord's vineyard; our minds, to think and act in the light of the Gospel; and especially to offer our hearts to love and to make choices in accordance with God's will. All this happens thanks to the working of the Holy Spirit. And in this way we become instruments in God's hands, so that Jesus can act in the world through us.

3. The third aspect is Mary's faith as a journey. The Council says that Mary "advanced in her pilgrimage of faith" (*Lumen gentium*, no. 58). In this way she precedes us on this pilgrimage; she accompanies and sustains us.

How was Mary's faith a journey? In the sense that her entire life was to follow her Son: he—Jesus—is the way, he is the path! To press forward in faith, to advance in the spiritual pilgrimage that is faith, is nothing other than to follow Jesus: to listen to him and be guided by his words; to see how he acts and to follow in his footsteps; to have his same sentiments.

And what are these sentiments of Jesus? Humility, mercy, closeness to others, but also a firm rejection of hypocrisy, duplicity, and idolatry. The way of Jesus is the way of a love that is faithful to the end, even to sacrificing one's life; it is the way of the cross. The journey of faith thus passes through the cross. Mary understood this from the beginning, when Herod sought to kill the newborn Jesus. But then this experience of the cross became deeper when Jesus was rejected. Mary was always with Jesus; she followed Jesus in the midst of the crowds, and she heard all the gossip and the nastiness of those who opposed the Lord. And she carried this cross! Mary's faith encountered misunderstanding and contempt—when Jesus' "hour" came, the hour of his Passion, when Mary's faith was a little flame burning in the night, a little light flickering in the darkness. Through the night of Holy Saturday,

Mary kept watch. Her flame, small but bright, remained burning until the dawn of the resurrection. And when she received word that the tomb was empty, her heart was filled with the joy of faith: Christian faith in the death and resurrection of Jesus Christ. Faith always brings us to joy, and Mary is the Mother of joy! May she teach us to take the path of joy, to experience this joy! That was the high point—this joy, this meeting of Jesus and Mary, and we can imagine what it was like. Their meeting was the high point of Mary's journey of faith, and that of the whole Church. What is our faith like? Like Mary, do we keep it burning even at times of difficulty, in moments of darkness? Do I feel the joy of faith?

39

Her Intercession

Evangelii gaudium, nos. 285–88, 24 November 2013

On the cross, when Jesus endured in his own flesh the dramatic encounter of the sin of the world and God's mercy, he could feel at his feet the consoling presence of his mother and his friend. At that crucial moment, before fully

> *Christ brought us to Mary because he did not want us to journey without a mother.*

accomplishing the work his Father had entrusted to him, Jesus said to Mary, "Woman, here is your son." Then he said to his beloved friend, "Here is your mother" (John 19:26–27). These words of the dying Jesus are not chiefly the expression of his devotion and concern for his mother; rather, they are a revelatory formula that manifests the mystery of a special saving mission. Jesus left us his mother to be *our* mother. Only after doing so did Jesus know that "all was now finished" (John 19:28). At the foot of the cross, at the supreme hour of the new creation, Christ led us to Mary. He brought us to her because he did not want us to journey without a mother, and our people read in this maternal image all the mysteries of the Gospel.

The Lord did not want to leave the Church without this icon of womanhood. Mary, who brought him into the world with great faith, also accompanies "the rest of her offspring, those who keep the commandments of God and bear testimony to Jesus" (Rev. 12:17). The close connection between Mary, the Church, and each member of the faithful, based on the fact that each in his or her own way brings forth Christ, has been beautifully expressed by Blessed Isaac of Stella: "In the inspired Scriptures, what is said in a universal sense of the virgin mother, the Church, is understood in an individual sense of the Virgin Mary . . . In a way, every Christian is also believed to be a bride of God's word, a mother of Christ, his daughter and sister, at once virginal and fruitful . . . Christ dwelt for nine months in the tabernacle of Mary's womb. He dwells until the end of the ages in the tabernacle of the Church's faith. He will dwell forever in the knowledge and love of each faithful soul."

Mary was able to turn a stable into a home for Jesus, with poor swaddling clothes and an abundance of love. She is the handmaid of the Father who sings his praises. She is the friend who is ever concerned that wine not be lacking in our lives. She is the woman whose heart was pierced by a sword and who understands all our pain. As mother of all, she is a sign of hope for people suffering the birth pangs of justice. She is the missionary who draws near to us and accompanies us throughout life, opening our hearts to faith by her maternal love. As a true mother, she walks at our side, she shares our struggles, and she constantly surrounds us with God's love. Through her many titles, often linked to her shrines, Mary shares the history of each people that has received the Gospel, and she becomes part of their historic identity. Many Christian parents ask that their children be baptized in a Marian shrine as a sign of their faith in her motherhood, which brings forth new children for God. There, in these many shrines, we can see how Mary brings together her children who with great effort come as pilgrims to see her and to be seen by her. Here they find strength from God to bear the weariness and the suffering in their lives. As she did with Juan Diego, Mary offers them maternal comfort and love, and whispers in their ear, "Let your heart not be troubled . . . Am I not here, who am your Mother?"

We ask the Mother of the living Gospel to intercede that this invitation to a new phase of evangelization will be accepted by the entire ecclesial community. Mary is the woman of faith, who lives and advances in faith, and "her exceptional pilgrimage of faith represents a constant point of reference for the Church." Mary let herself be guided by the Holy Spirit on a journey of faith toward a destiny of service and fruitfulness. Today we look to her and ask her to help us proclaim the message of salvation to all and to enable new disciples to become evangelizers in turn. Along this journey of evangelization we will have our moments of aridity, darkness, and even fatigue. Mary herself experienced these things during the years of Jesus' childhood in Nazareth: "This is the beginning of the Gospel, the joyful good news. However, it is not difficult to see in that beginning a particular heaviness of heart, linked with a sort of night of faith—to use the words of St. John of the Cross—a kind of 'veil' through which one has to draw near to the Invisible One and to live in intimacy with the mystery. And this is the way that Mary, for many years, lived in intimacy with the mystery of her Son, and went forward in her pilgrimage of faith."

There is a Marian "style" to the Church's work of evangelization. Whenever we look to Mary, we come to believe once again in the revolutionary nature of love and tenderness. In her we see that humility and tenderness are not virtues of the weak but of the strong, who need not treat others poorly in order to feel important

> *Whenever we look to Mary, we come to believe once again in the revolutionary nature of love and tenderness.*

themselves. Contemplating Mary, we realize that she who praised God for "bringing down the mighty from their thrones" and "sending the rich away empty" (Luke 1:52–53) is also the one who brings a homely warmth to our pursuit of justice. She is also the one who carefully keeps "all these things, pondering them in her heart" (Luke 2:19).

Mary is able to recognize the traces of God's Spirit in events great and small. She constantly contemplates the mystery of God in our world, in human history, and in our daily lives. She is the woman of prayer and work in Nazareth, and she is also Our Lady of Help, who sets out from her town "with haste" (Luke 1:39) to be of service to others. This interplay of justice and tenderness, of contemplation and concern for others, is what makes the ecclesial community look to Mary as a model of evangelization. We implore her maternal intercession that the Church may become a home for many peoples, a mother for all peoples, and that the way may be opened to the birth of a new world. It is the risen Christ who tells us, with a power that fills us with confidence and unshakeable hope: "Behold, I make all things new" (Rev. 21:5). With Mary we advance confidently toward the fulfillment of this promise.

Essential Chronology of
POPE FRANCIS'S *Life*

1936
17 December Born Jorge Mario Bergoglio in Buenos Aires into a family originally from Marche (Italy) who had immigrated to Argentina. Mario, his father, was an accountant in the railway company; Regina Sivori, his mother, was a homemaker. Jorge was the first of five children; his siblings are Óscar, Marta, Alberto, and María Elena.

1957
After achieving his diploma in chemistry, chose to become a priest and started seminary in Villa Devoto.

1960
12 March Took his first vows.

1963
After completing humanities studies in Santiago, Chile, returned to Argentina, earning his philosophy degree at San José College in San Miguel.

1970
Finished his theological studies and graduated from San José College.

1930	1950	1960	1970

1958
11 March Started his novitiate at the Society of Jesus.

1964–66
Taught literature and psychology, first in Santa Fé and then in Buenos Aires.

1969
13 December Ordained a priest.

1973
22 April Made his perpetual profession.

31 July After having been consultor, became provincial superior of Argentina's Jesuits.

1992

20 May After Bergoglio served for several years as spiritual director and confessor, John Paul II appointed him auxiliary bishop of Buenos Aires. Worked closely with Cardinal Antonio Quarracino, from whom he received episcopal ordination (27 June). Chose as his motto *Miserando atque eligendo* ("Having mercy, He chose him") and inserted the Christogram IHS, symbol of the Society of Jesus, into his coat of arms.

2001

21 February Created a cardinal by John Paul II.

2013

11 February Benedict XVI announced he would relinquish the Petrine ministry at the end of the month.

13 March Elected the new supreme pontiff, choosing the name *Francis*—he is the first Latin American pope, the first Jesuit pope, and the first to take the name *Francis*.

7 April Took his seat as Bishop of Rome on the Cathedra Romana.

24 June Created a pontifical commission to investigate the Institute for Works of Religion (the Vatican Bank).

29 June First encyclical *Lumen fidei* published, thus completing the document Benedict XVI bequeathed to him.

8 July Made a historic visit to the island of Lampedusa.

1980   **1990**   **2000**   **2010**

1980

Appointed rector of San José College, where he worked until 1986, when he stepped down to study theology in Germany and research Romano Guardini for his doctoral dissertation. His studies in Germany were interrupted by a summons from his superiors in Argentina to take up higher positions. Ministered as a priest in a parish in Córdoba.

1993

21 December Appointed vicar general of the archdiocese of Buenos Aires.

1997

3 June Promoted to coadjutor archbishop of Buenos Aires. Upon Cardinal Quarracino's death a year later, succeeded him in leading the archdiocese (28 February) and became the primate of Argentina.

2005

Took part in the conclave electing Benedict XVI.

2013

22–29 July Took part in World Youth Day in Rio de Janeiro, Brazil.

22 September Pastoral visit to Cagliari.

28 September Established the Council of Cardinals, tasked with advising Francis on ruling the Universal Church and starting reorganization of the apostolic constitution *Pastor bonus*, regarding the role of the Roman Curia.

4 October Made pastoral visit to Assisi.

24 November Apostolic exhortation *Evangelii gaudium* published.

2014

22 February Summoned a consistory for the creation of new cardinals.

List of Sources

1. "The Embrace of God's Mercy": Homily for the Mass for the Possession of the Chair of Bishop of Rome, 7 April 2013 (www.vatican.va).

2. "The Light of Faith": *Lumen fidei*, nos. 4 and 34, 29 June 2013 (www.vatican.va).

3. "The Christian Message": Homily for the Easter Vigil, 30 March 2013 (www.vatican.va).

4. "The Revolution of Freedom": Address to the Participants in the Ecclesial Convention of the Diocese of Rome, 17 June 2013 (www.vatican.va).

5. "Being with Christ": Address to the Participants at the International Congress on Catechesis, 27 September 2013 (www.vatican.va).

6. "Listen to the Cry of the Poor": *Evangelii gaudium*, nos. 186–88, 198, 24 November 2013 (www.vatican.va).

7. "A House of Communion": General Audience, 25 November 2013 (www.vatican.va).

8. "A House That Welcomes All": General Audience, 2 October 2013 (www.vatican.va).

9. "A House of Harmony": General Audience, 9 October 2013 (www.vatican.va).

10. "Sent to Bring the Gospel to All the World": General Audience, 16 October 2013 (www.vatican.va).

11. "Be Guided by the Holy Spirit": General Audience, 15 May 2013 (www.vatican.va).

12. "Good News, Harmony, Mission": Homily on the Solemnity of Pentecost, 19 May 2013 (www.vatican.va).

13. "Do Not Be Afraid": *Regina Coeli*, 14 April 2013 (www.vatican.va).

14. "Bringing the Word of God": Homily for the Mass in the Basilica of St. Paul Outside the Walls, 14 April 2013 (www.vatican.va).

15. "Called to Proclaim the Gospel": Homily for the Mass with the Brazilian Bishops, 27 Jul 2013 (www.vatican.va).

16. "Conveying Hope and Joy": Homily at the Basilica of the Shrine of Our Lady of the Conception of Aparecida, 24 July 2013 (www.vatican.va).

17. "Giving All": Homily at the Profession of Faith with the Bishops of the Italian Episcopal Conference, 23 May 2013 (www.vatican.va).

18. "Coming Out of Ourselves": General Audience, 27 March 2013 (www.vatican.va).

19. "Walking": Address to the Clergy in the Cathedral of San Rufino in Assisi, 4 October (www.vatican.va).

20. "Taking the Cross": Homily on Palm Sunday, 24 March 2013 (www.vatican.va).

21. "Evangelizing": General Audience, 22 May 2013 (www.vatican.va).

22. "To Be a Pastor": Address to a Group of Newly Appointed Bishops Taking Part in a Conference, 19 September 2013 (www.vatican.va).

23. "Priests Who Come to Serve": Homily, 21 April 2013 (www.vatican.va).

24. "The Anointing of the People": Homily at the Chrism Mass, 28 March 2013 (www.vatican.va).

25. "To the Outskirts of Existence": Address to the Lay Movements on Pentecost Vigil, 18 May 2013 (www.vatican.va).

26. "Hospitality and Service": Address to the Missionaries of the Homeless Shelter Dono di Maria, 21 May 2013 (www.vatican.va).

27. "Refugees and Those Uprooted from Life": Address to the Participants in the Plenary of the Pontifical Council for the Pastoral Care of Migrants and Itinerant People, 24 May 2013 (www.vatican.va).

28. "A Culture of Solidarity": Address at the Astalli Centre, the Jesuit Refugee Service in Rome, 10 September 2013 (www.vatican.va).

29. "The Logic of Power and Violence": Homily at the Vigil of Prayer for Peace, 7 September 2013 (www.vatican.va).

30. "The Cult of the God of Money": General Audience, 5 June 2013 (www.vatican.va).

31. "The Leprosy of Careerism": Address to the Community of the Pontifical Ecclesiastical Academy, 6 June 2013 (www.vatican.va).

32. "Undressing the Spirit of the World": Speech in the Room of Renunciation in the Archbishop's Residence, 4 October 2013 (www.vatican.va).

33. "Free to Choose Good": Address to the Students of the Jesuit Schools, 7 June 2013 (www.vatican.va).

34. "The Hunger for Dignity": Address to the Community of Varginha, 25 July 2013 (www.vatican.va).

35. "The Commitment to Peace": Address to the Participants in the International Meeting for Peace Sponsored by the Community of Sant'Egidio, 30 September 2013 (www.vatican.va).

36. "For a New Solidarity": Address to the Centesimus Annus Pro Pontifice Foundation, 25 May 2013 (www.vatican.va).

37. "Her Example": Address at the End of the Marian Month of May, 31 Ma 2013 (www.vatican.va).

38. "Her Faith": Prayer for the Marian Day, 12 October 2013 (www.vatican.va).

39. "Her Intercession": *Evangelii gaudium*, nos. 285–88, 24 November 2013 (www.vatican.va).

A Young Woman Lives
Out the Call for Mercy

Mercy in the City
How to Feed the Hungry, Give Drink to the Thirsty,
Visit the Imprisoned, and Keep Your Day Job

Kerry Weber

Pb • 3892-5 • $13.95

Mercy in the City is Kerry Weber's story of
exploring the challenges and rewards that
accompany a lay Catholic trying to practice
the Seven Corporal Works of Mercy in
New York City.

To order: call 800-621-1008, visit www.loyolapress.com/mercy, or visit your local bookseller.

An Invitation to Encounter
Christ in a Whole New Way

Under the Influence of Jesus
The Transforming Experience
of Encountering Christ

Joe Paprocki

Pb • 4050-8 • $15.95

In *Under the Influence of Jesus*, best-selling
author Joe Paprocki explores the particular
characteristics of a changed heart and life that
result from accepting Jesus' message. *Under the
Influence of Jesus* is ultimately an invitation to
encounter Christ in a whole new way, to thrive
under his lordship, and to use our own transformed hearts and lives to
help bring others into a life-changing relationship with Jesus.

To order: call 800-621-1008, visit www.loyolapress.com/undertheinfluence,
or visit your local bookseller.

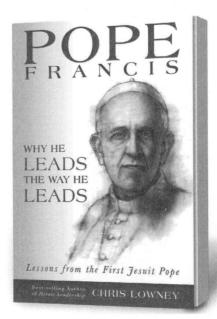